SOUL SCENTS: AWAKEN

Paula Moldenhauer

SOUL SCENTS: AWAKEN

Paula Moldenhauer

Soul Scents Publishing
www.soulscents.us

Soul Scents Publishing

Soul Scents: Awaken A Spiritual Journey in the Son's Embrace

Print ISBN-13: 978-1522759683
Print ISBN-10: 1522759689

Artwork:
~ Lisa-Joy, www.facebook.com/lisajoyart

~ Cover Design:
Kim Liddiard of the Creative Pixel,
www.thecreativepixel.com

Project Management:
~ Carmen Barber, KeepingYouWriting@gmail.com

Editor:
~ Ruth Meyers

Scripture quotations marked KJV are taken from the King James Version of the Bible.

Scripture quotations marked NKJV are taken from the New King James Version®. Copyright © 1982 by Thomas Nelson, Inc. Used by permission. All rights reserved.

Scripture quotations marked NIV are taken from the HOLY BIBLE, NEW INTERNATIONAL VERSION®. NIV®. Copyright © 1973, 1978, 1984, 2011 by Biblica, Inc.™ Used by permission. All rights reserved worldwide.

Scripture quotations marked MSG are from THE MESSAGE. Copyright © by Eugene H. Peterson 1993, 1994, 1995, 1996, 2000, 2001, 2002. Used by permission of NavPress Publishing Group.Scripture quotations marked NLT are taken from the Holy Bible. New Living Translation copyright© 1996, 2004, 2007 by Tyndale House Foundation. Used by permission of Tyndale House Publishers, Inc. Carol Stream, Illinois 60188. All rights reserved.

Scripture quotations marked CEV are from the Contemporary English Version, Copyright © 1995 by American Bible Society. Used by permission.

Scripture quotations marked NASB are taken from the New American Standard Bible, © 1960, 1962, 1963, 1968, 1971, 1972, 1973, 1975, 1977, 1995 by The Lockman Foundation. Used by permission.

Scripture quotations marked AMP are taken from the Amplified® Bible, © 1954, 1958, 1962, 1964, 1965, 1987 by The Lockman Foundation. Used by permission.

Scripture quotations marked TLB are taken from The Living Bible © 1971. Used by permission of Tyndale House Publishers, Inc. Wheaton, Illinois 60189. All rights reserved.

Dedication

Dedicated to my Best Friend—the King of Kings and
Lord of Lords—who continually sets my heart free by
His grace and to all those who've prayed this book into
publication, especially my sweet husband, Jerry.

Contents

A Note from the Author

Dear Friend,

It is with great joy I offer you the ramblings of my heart—a heart which has panted after God, whined before Him, agonized at His ways, and danced in joy. This volume of *Soul Scents* is the first of four. The devotions written in the complete set were penned over a span of more than ten years. If you choose to join me for all four sets we'll journey together with Christ for an entire year, but what you will read will be a saga of a much longer slice of my life. I offer it to you in hopes my path, which has been both glorious and rugged, will offer you joy, peace, and nuggets of truth as you journey on your own.

Our precious Lord met me time and again, making the brightest of days more delightful and never forsaking me even when I railed at Him in my darkest hours. As a teen I loved the old saying, "A friend divides your sorrow and doubles your joy." It is easy to say our Jesus is exactly that kind of Friend.

It's interesting as I edited the portions which I wrote many years ago that those devotions required very little conceptual change. Some of the prayers seemed much more risky than they did when I first wrote them, and some of my declarations felt a little naive from this side, ten years later. But none of it rang untrue. Back then I simply didn't understand how deeply the truths would be tested or how fully some of those prayers would be answered.

As I write today I'm in the joyful anticipation of a new season, convinced (most days at least) that God is unfolding a flourishing life of living in productive freedom with Him. But the volumes of this year of *Soul Scents* devotionals walk through many seasons, which I've named from this side of the journey as I ponder the eras that resulted in the words you are about to read. The *Soul Scents* collection is made of four volumes: *Awaken, Rooted, Bloom,* and *Flourish*. While all of the volumes contain some updated content as well as devotionals written long ago, I gave the collection a bit of its own story arch. I hope this spiritual unfolding will bless and encourage you as you ponder your own spiritual progression.

While *Soul Scents* can be read in any order and at any time of the year, if you choose to begin *Awaken* in January and follow the other volumes through for the whole year you will discover I've endeavored to match some of the devotions to the time of year, which means each volume connects at some level to the seasons and church calendar. (For example the last volume, *Flourish*, contains thoughts which are easily applied to Thanksgiving, Advent, and Christ's Birth.) *Soul Scents* offers thematic thoughts for each week of the year and is broken into five devotionals, one for each weekday. I've found in my own devotional life that rhythms are different on the weekend, so I left two days a week open to allow for other choices or to catch up during particularly busy times.

Thanks to the talented Lisa-Joy we have a little gift for

you in the paper edition of *Soul Scents* devotionals. You may have noticed that coloring books for adults are now best-sellers. Adults are discovering that coloring helps them relax, embrace creativity, and even focus on spiritual connection with God. For this reason, the four seasons tree Lisa-Joy designed for *Soul Scents* appears each week in black and white form. As you ponder the concepts you've read, consider pulling out some colored pencils. I'll bet each week's tree will express something different as you take the time to color and see how the Lord is reaching out to you. There is also a free coloring page at the back of each volume for you to enjoy.

Another devotional tool I hope you'll utilize if you're using the print version of this devotional is the white space within the devotional weeks. Depending on the length of the daily reading there is often room to jot notes, doodle, or write your own prayer. I encourage you to interact with God and this content however you feel led and to do so right on the pages of the book.

Over these many years as an author I have prayed not only for my journey, but also for the spiritual formation of my readers. I ask Him again today to meet you where you are, to shower you with grace and love, and to set you free to live a life of flourishing, productive freedom in Him. I am humbled and excited you've chosen to take this journey with me as we rest in the Son's embrace. I love to hear from my readers. You may contact me at: Paula@paulamoldenhauer.com. May God bless us all!

Week One ~ Unveiling True Desire

Week One ~ Unveiling True Desire

Day 1: Fragrance

I am grateful that God always makes it possible for Christ to lead us to victory. God also helps us spread the knowledge about Christ everywhere, and this knowledge is like the smell of perfume.
    ~ 2 Corinthians 2:14 (CEV)

The bleak grays and dull browns of winter pushed away the sunshine, and my mood matched the dismal day.

It was a small thing really—an expected $20 that never appeared. It wasn't as though I needed it to feed the family or keep the electricity on. I just wanted it for me. It'd been a long time since I'd had the money to treat myself to my favorite store—one that sold scented body wash and lotions. I had a best-loved fragrance that came out every year or two—Sugar Plum Spice. I dreamed of splashing it all over me in the shower and then smoothing the luxurious scent into my arms, legs, and feet. I could almost—not quite—smell it, the fragrance of magical moments. I'd wear it to special events, like our annual New Year's Eve party, or simply as a daily treat. I dreamed of it for weeks, expecting a monetary gift in the mail.

The anticipated card arrived offering sweet

sentiments but no check so I could indulge in sweet smells. It seemed another blow in the long season of unmet expectations and empty coffers. I felt silly to be discouraged over such a little thing—but I grieved the lack.

In my women's Bible study group the leader challenged us to a new way of thinking. She said to look underneath every desire to find a deeper longing—a longing for Christ. I talked to the Lord about the scented lotion.

"Ever wonder how I smell? Breathe deeply," He whispered to my heart.

I searched the Scriptures for more of Him as I mediated on the thought that His aroma must be lovelier than anything I'd ever smelled. I was reminded that Paul says God leads us "along in Christ's triumphal procession," and "uses us to spread the knowledge of Christ everywhere, like a sweet perfume" (2 Corinthians 2:14, NLT).

I asked the Lord to let me know Him so deeply that His smell rubbed off on me and lingered in the air around me. I didn't need Sugar Plum Spice. I needed to know more of Him.

How about you? Do you long to experience Him more intimately?

I invite you to come with me on a new journey to discover the wonders of Jesus—His grace, His love, His wisdom, and His beauty. We won't run out of places to explore together as we seek Him. He is beyond finding out!

Let's hang out with Him. Think about Him. Talk to Him.

I'll be vulnerable with my journey in hopes being real will help us let go of the pretense of religion and grab hold of the glory of relationship with God. I pray the Lord uses this time together to pull us more deeply into His heart of grace. Through the power of His Holy Spirit, you and I walk forward with a whiff of His sweet scent lingering behind us.

Jesus, I bravely step onto this path into Your heart. Reveal who You truly are. Open my mind to understand You, my heart to feel You, even my very senses to discover You. I want to catch a whiff of Your fragrance, to see You with new eyes, to feel Your touch, to taste Your goodness—and to leave that beautiful Christ aroma trailing after me for others to sniff.

Week One ~ Unveiling True Desire

Day 2: Longing for Community

I pray that they will all be one, just as you and I are one—as you are in me, Father, and I am in you. And may they be in us so that the world will believe you sent me.
    ~ John 17:21 (NLT)

It was a season of discovering deepest longings and reshaping schemata for life. The set-up for the journey started in the spring when God called us away from our church family. I resigned my part-time job there, not knowing that my husband's job would come to an end the next month. Before we had time to find work or a new church my husband's father suffered a heart attack. We drove miles to be with family and spent a month watching my father-in-law die. We came home with aching hearts to no income, no church family, a pile of bills, and a broken freezer full of spoiled meat. As October's leaves twirled to the ground, my emotions swirled with them into brittle, lifeless discouragement.

Little did I know that the Lord was taking me on a journey to awaken my heart. There were areas of it I had shut down—longings I suppressed, desires I ignored—all in the name of holiness. (Or at least in the name of survival.) God wanted my heart to be awakened—alive to Him. That included being honest with my dreams and desires. The Lord probed into my deepest longings, including my craving for a church family. As He revealed the desire I embraced it, but week after week we'd try a new church only to return home discouraged and lonely.

My children grieved their friends, the music, and the children's classes of our old church. My husband searched for a place that embraced the grace of Christ. I wanted a safe community where I could share my aching heart in genuine friendship and grow alongside honest, vulnerable people. The hurt of not finding a church where we belonged pressed upon us, but God called me to embrace the pain instead of suppressing it.

Slowly God revealed a deeper desire—the desire for community with Him. He pointed me to the perfect community Jesus experiences with His Father and shares with the Holy Spirit. Jesus invited me into community with the Three in One in His beautiful prayer, "Father, make them one, even as You and I are one."

I'm learning the ability to have deep, trusted community with others grows as I discover the perfect community of the Trinity. He lives with Himself without jealousy or strife in harmony of spirit and purpose, even though Father, Son, and Holy Spirit have different functions. It is in the community of God's fellowship I am treated with such loving care that I gain courage to be vulnerable with others. As I receive His grace, I learn to offer it. As I am filled up with His love, I love more freely.

Holy God, Three in One, reveal Yourself and what it is like to live in the kind of community You enjoy. Remove jealousy and strife from my relationships. Show me how fully You love and teach me to love others that way. Bind me to Yourself in perfect harmony of purpose and help me and those I'm in community with to walk together with that same Oneness of spirit and goal.

Day 3: Alive to Beauty

You listen to the longings of those who suffer. You offer them hope, and you pay attention to their cries for help.
~ Psalm 10:17 (CEV)

Sometimes it's hard to get over the disappointments of the holidays. Maybe you're thinking about that today—how the old year ended in longing without the fulfillment of your hopes. I've been there. Thanksgiving starts it all, and then you face a whole month of longing—for people, for things, for a heart that can celebrate.

Thanksgiving the year of my father-in-law's death brought visions of community, piles of good food, and homey warmth. I accepted the fact we had neither time nor money to travel to be with extended family and embraced the joy of having my mother-in-law in town, praying we'd all survive this first Thanksgiving without my father-in-law. Eagerly I invited some friends over—a family like us who had no one in town to share the day with.

As I allowed my heart to come alive I discovered a craving for a beautifully set table—matching glassware, my grandmother's china, new linens in the warm browns and greens of Thanksgiving, and a centerpiece with round, orange pumpkins. I longed to bring beauty into my grieving world and to share beauty with my family and friends.

I couldn't afford the dream, but it grew within me. Determined, I made a trip to the secondhand store. I fingered the used tablecloths, finding some that would create just the ambiance I desired. I carried my selections to the cashier, and my eyes widened as she rang them up.

I couldn't even create my dreams at the thrift store.

Laying the linens aside I went home and collapsed into heaving sobs. My wavering faith vacillated between accusing God of abandoning me to clinging desperately to Him.

I had a choice: shut down again or continue the awakening process. Killing desire was self-preservation, but I was tired of not really living. I prayed God would show me how to keep my heart awake in times of pain and disappointment. I wrote in my journal. "My real self, the life I am meant to live—a soul alive that awakens beauty in the hearts of those around me—that life—that me—disappears when I enter self-preservation."

That was years ago, but even now it sometimes feels easier to pretend I don't have need than to enter into disappointment. I get tired of hurting. I get tired of being still before God and allowing Him to reveal the deeper longings of my heart.

Sometimes killing my heart isn't such an obvious choice. It happens gradually as commitments, disappointments, and busyness creep over me. Then one day I wake up and realize that I'm just surviving again, existing, not living.

John Eldredge, in the book *Waking the Dead*, encourages readers to ask God what is needed to care for their hearts. I have a vivid memory of how beautifully and simply God answered this prayer one day when the children were little and I was overwhelmed with the demands of homeschooling. I awoke dreading another day of the grind. When I admitted my feelings to the Lord and asked Him how to care for my heart and the hearts of my children, I felt a whisper inside, "do school at the park." We left the familiar four walls behind and spent a glorious day in the sunshine. All of us came home renewed.

Have you thought recently about the things that touch your heart? What is it that makes you feel alive inside? What opens your soul to experience God's beauty? What disappointments might have deeper longings that can be answered in Him? Ask Him to show you, and then embrace His answer.

Taking care of your heart is never wasted time.

Jesus, sometimes my heart feels dead inside. I shut down desires rather than face disappointment. Daily routines suck the life from me. Help me not to shut down my heart. I want to live beyond self-preservation. Please teach me how. Open my soul to experience Your beauty. Awaken my heart to joy. Teach me to dance in Your green pastures even on the cloudy sky days.

Week One ~ Unveiling True Desire
Day 4: Does Your Mouth Water?

Taste and see that the Lord is good. Oh, the joys of those who take refuge in him!
~ Psalm 34:8 (NLT)

My mouth watered as I walked through the store seeing the chocolates perched on the shelf. It was time for COSTCO's annual display of chocolates from around the world. I imagined the taste of raspberry centers surrounded by rich, dark chocolate. I paused, then to the dismay of my children and my own heart, I twirled the shopping cart toward the toilet paper aisle.

There it was again. The desire seemed simple enough—but there was no money. Even the flour and toilet paper brought more debt. I drove home with an empty ache. I'd admitted another desire only to have it fly in my face. It seemed such a small thing—but even small things can be big when piled on top of each other.

I mentioned earlier this week that we'd left our church and our jobs, had little money, and then lost my husband's father. Added to the grief was the serious illness of a loved one and the divorce of my mom and stepdad. Later that year I realized why our financial stress felt so great. That year our income was only $10,000. Now, if we lived on a farm in the Dakotas we could maybe find a way to make that livable, but we live in a big city where the cost of living is high. Furthermore, my husband and I raised four wonderful children, which means four growing bodies consuming amazing quantity of foods and constantly needing new shoes and jeans! When I talk about little things like the lack of scented lotion or candy, it seems so trivial — but it was the cry of a heart that was experiencing much lack. There were other things pressing upon me — things too deeply personal to share here.

I spent much of that season curled in our country blue recliner with my Bible and journal open on my lap. It was during one of those times the Lord spoke to me about the candies. My mouth watered. I could taste the bittersweet of European chocolate.

"Taste and see that the Lord is good." His presence flooded me as my heart leapt within. I searched my concordance for the reference of the scripture dancing through my mind. I found it in Psalm 34:8, "Taste and see that the Lord is good; blessed is the man who takes refuge in him" (NIV).

I don't share our struggles to gain sympathy. I share because the lacks I experienced were the impetus to discovering the deepest cry of my heart: to know Jesus more intimately.

It is easy to enjoy the goodies of life and never find the best of life: Him. What felt like His withholding was really my Lord offering of the greatest gift of all.

Himself.

Precious Jesus, Reveal Yourself to me in my desires. Don't let me be satisfied with only the gifts of Your hand. Open my heart to the greatest gift of all: You. Let me receive the good in this world as a reflection of Your goodness. Let me taste and see that You are good.

Week One ~ Unveiling True Desire

Day 5: Reflecting the Sparkle

Your instructions are more valuable to me than millions in gold and silver.
   ~ Psalm 119:72 (NLT)

It was a season of lack and a season of fullness as God taught me to look for Him beneath my desires. Materially, there was much lack (as an American can know lack), but spiritually there was plenty. As the Lord peeled back the layers of desire to reveal Himself, I walked forward in the joyful knowledge of His personal attention.

I'd stand at the store wanting to spend indulgently. "Spend yourself indulgently," He whispered, "for whoever loses his life for my sake will gain it."

I sat at the computer, my fingers aching to create. I longed to produce beautiful words, flowing together in a life rhythm of their own. "You are my letter," He gently reminded me, "written that all may see and believe."

As I stood on wobbly feet, learning how to look underneath my longings to discover the desire for Him, another hurt hurled at me. Someone came into our home and took most of my jewelry. Much of it had sentimental value.

"How could you, God?" Inwardly I stomped my feet. "How could you let them? Especially now?"

I searched my Bible for comfort and found new meaning in His admonition to store up for myself treasure in heaven instead of on earth where thieves break in and steal. When I calmed I asked God how to be content with my circumstances and keep my heart alive when what little I had was stolen away.

I probed my desire to wear pretty, sparkling jewelry searching for a desire for Him. I found my deeper desire was to be truly coordinated and put together on the inside—beautiful where it counted. Weary of the fight to overcome inner ugliness, I wanted my private self to match my public self.

"Lord," I whispered, "I want to sparkle with the beauty of You. If You put that inside me, thieves can't steal the shimmer."

Each morning I dressed and reached, out of habit, for jewelry that wasn't there. I'd turn away. There was still an ache, but most mornings God replaced it with a song. As I finished my morning toiletries, I hummed, "Lord, you are more precious silver . . . and nothing I desire compares with You."

What lack in your life reveals an aching longing? Won't you join me on the journey to discover your truest desire?

Lord, You are the only thing that deeply satisfies. Reveal Yourself to me as I am honest about my desires. As I focus on You, remake me to reflect Your sparkle.

Awaken

Week Two ~ Joining the Dance

Week Two ~ Joining the Dance

Day 1: His Deep Care

Then Jesus wept.
> *~ John 11:35 (NLT)*

Barren branches stretched toward a gray sky. The grass, brown and brittle, contributed to my sense of a dry, stark winter. The mound of grief within only accentuated my perception.

As I grieved I rejected the idea that God could grieve with me. I couldn't stand the thought of Him crying over our hurts. That would mean He would have continuous grief as He looked over His creation.

One night the Holy Spirit broke through the lies I'd believed and revealed the truth. God grieved with me. I sobbed, unable to grasp how the King of the Universe could enter into the massive pain His creation walked through daily.

The next morning I prayed about God's grief, and He revealed the deeper reason I rejected the idea of Him grieving. I'd asked to know Him more. I wanted to know the beauty, the joy, and the wonder of Him. But entering more deeply into His heart also meant sharing His pain.

I didn't want that part.

He also showed me that it scared me to see God as emotional. If He grieved and cried with us did that mean He was unstable, untrustworthy? I compared God to people I knew whose emotions were out of control. Lack of ability to handle pain, anger, fear, and disappointment made them a threat to my emotional safety. Was God like that?

Thankfully, God showed me His emotions of pain were not to be feared. I came to understand that because He loved me, He grieved with me.

Author Larry Crabb wrote in the book *Shattered Dreams* that it is a little like taking your baby for first immunizations.

I remember taking our first child, Sarah, in for her shots. Her trusting eyes looked at me with the shock of betrayal as the nurse jabbed her with the needle. I cried with my baby as the nurse told her, "Your mommy didn't do that to you, honey." I could have protected Sarah from the momentary pain of the needle, but I felt the greater danger was the disease the immunization fought, so I allowed my sweet baby to hurt.

I still remember the look of disbelief and betrayal in my sweet girl's eyes. I've looked at God with that same expression.

As a mom I must have felt a bit of what God feels when He allows pain in our lives for our own good. At any minute He could stop it. He could step right in and take away the things that wound us, but like a parent who allows the needle of immunizations for a higher purpose He allows the punctures of life we must endure for our emotional and spiritual health.

With that thought in mind, it's easy to see God grieving with me, crying with me, and holding me close. He chooses to enter my grief so I can find ultimate healing, His loving tears a balm to my wounds.

Maybe you've already grasped this beautiful truth— the God of the universe is right there with you, sharing the pain you carry today. Lean into Him, my friend. Let's rest in our Father's embrace, trusting Him to give us only His best care.

Jesus, thank You for loving me enough to grieve with me. In my seasons of grief help me to allow myself as many tears as I need. Hold me close as I cry and reveal Yourself to me. I trust You are doing what You do best, lovingly bandaging my aching heart and, in Your time and way, re-creating beauty out of pain.

Week Two ~ Joining the Dance

Day 2: The Cobbler

Dance! Dance!
Beautiful woman from Shulam, let us see you dance!
~ Song of Solomon 6:13 (CEV)

Its sheer beauty overwhelmed me. The music of the
symphony reached like long, melodic fingers probing my
heart. Somehow it wasn't just another educational field trip.
As the music swelled my eyes filled. I sat, entranced, as a
deep longing rose within me. I wanted to experience such
beauty and then create it to share with others. My heart
opened to the Spirit as He used the deep bass of the tuba and
the lilting melodies of the flutes to get my attention.

I leaned forward as they played a song based on a
book written by a fifth grader in Denver and put to music by
a cellist in the symphony. The brimming tears began to flow,
in little rivulets, down my cheeks. See, the cobbler in the
story didn't know how to dance. The whole village loved a
jig, but the cobbler was kept so busy mending their shoes
that he never learned.

One especially gorgeous day the mayor canceled

normal business so the villagers could celebrate the beautiful day by dancing together. The whole village population met in the streets—except the cobbler. His hammering could be heard in the distance. With all that dancing he had a lot of shoes to mend! A little boy who played violin heard the cobbler working and asked permission to go and get him for the dance.

When it was granted, he went to the cobbler and played for him. The busy cobbler didn't stop to listen, but, against his will, his feet started tapping. In frustration he told the boy he didn't know how to dance. The boy slowed the music so the cobbler could learn. When the cobbler grasped the skill, the boy ushered him out to the waiting village where all the inhabitants burst into cheers.

My tears flowed because I was the cobbler.

God called me to dance. There was much I hadn't yet discovered—beautiful, joyful, and creative things. The Lord wanted to free me to discover Him and through that discovery become who He created me to be.

Too busy fixing shoes, narrowly focused on the tasks and struggles of life, I didn't notice. There were shoes of my pain, shoes belonging to loved ones, shoes I picked up at church or in my work—and they were in the way. I couldn't rest in His grace or dance in the wonder of it.

I was working too hard at life.

What about you, my friend? Do you miss out on the beauty in life because your head is bent over the cobbler's bench? Is there a piece inside of you begging for release? Do your toes long to tap out an unexplored tune?

Join with me in asking our Creator to free us to be all He meant us to be. He's willing to slow the music so we can learn the dance of His grace.

Oh, Jesus! How often do You invite me to dance while I'm so busy working I don't even notice? Sometimes I'm afraid I don't even know how to dance. Help me lift my eyes from toiling so that I can see Your invitation. Help me to trust You to lead me and teach me the steps. I know You won't ask me to move to a rhythm beyond my ability. And, Lord? Someday I'd like dancing to be completely effortless in You.

Week Two ~ Joining the Dance

Day 3: Do You Want Me?

Come, let us worship and bow down.
Let us kneel before the Lord our maker,
For he is our God.
We are the people he watches over,
the flock under his care.
~ Psalm 95:6–7 (NLT)

The snow falling outside my kitchen window seemed as endless as my tears. I hadn't wanted to talk with anyone, but maybe it was good my friend knew what I was going through. She promised if I couldn't handle my commitment to teach classes the next week she'd teach for me. I walked to the bathroom, stared into the mirror at my red-rimmed eyes, and grimaced.

The preceding fall God taught me to look underneath my desires for the deepest desire of all, Him. He promised me that during this difficult time He was doing what was best for me.

That didn't change how hard it felt.

I cut back on responsibilities hoping I could refuel

and pick them up again. Instead, I seemed to reach the end of my resources. My endless prayers changed none of my circumstances.

Late one night in the silence of a sleeping household, I sat alone in my blue recliner reading *Shattered Dreams* by Larry Crabb and journaling. The Lord spoke to my heart, "What if I never give you the things you're asking Me for? Do you still want Me?"

Did I?

My breath caught in my throat.

Did I still want Him if He didn't make my life easier? Did I still want Him if He didn't give me my way? Did I want His gifts or His person?

His direct, simple question stopped me short—but I knew the answer.

"I want you, Lord. No matter what."

Instantly, the hopelessness in my heart shifted to quietness. I stood and put a worship song on my CD player. As the music swelled I raised my hands to Him, grasping a piece of the magnitude of His Deity. He was truly King of all, worthy beyond anything.

I swept across the room and then bowed before Him. My dance of surrender ended on my knees as I again offered God the throne of my heart—the throne I'd given Him years before. The profound, humble worship rising within was deeper than I'd ever known. Perhaps I felt it so intimately because I gave Him claim to protected parts within me— places I hadn't realized I'd withheld.

Since that time I've often asked myself if I want Him or the gifts from His hand. Beside my computer hangs a quote from *Letters to the Thirsty* by Ed Miller. "I have set my heart to know the LORD, not His plan, or some creedal

statement about Him, or even the many mercies that flow
freely from His hand. Himself I now desire, and nothing
else."

What is your heart set upon?

*Oh Father! In Your grace retrain my heart to thirst first and
foremost after You! When disappointments come help me to grieve
them, then release them to Your care. Hold me close. Reveal
Yourself that I may weather all life throws my way and never miss
the most beautiful gift of all—living close to You. I give You the
throne of my life knowing there will be times other idols will creep
in again. Please topple them every time. You alone are High King.*

Week Two ~ Joining the Dance

Day 4: You Might Just Learn to Dance

So if the Son makes you free, you will be free indeed.
~ John 8:36 (NASB)

The strands of "It Is Well with My Soul" flowed through the sanctuary and waltzed into my heart. In autumn I had felt crushed and broken, like brittle leaves that crackle underfoot. As winter began, the fallen leaves in my heart were blanketed by the clean white of surrender.

I'd learned (at least at a rudimentary level) to seek God for Himself, not just as Someone to fix the things in my life that I didn't like.

Yes! It was well with my soul!

I stood and sang with a free heart.

When the preacher spoke, my eyes were drawn to a different verse in the passage he referred to. It spoke about God casting down idols. As I read, I knew my season of pain had a purpose. My King had chosen it to cast down the idols of my heart.

I'd held onto many idols—idols of relationship, money, comfort, and ease. The biggest idol to topple was what I called the idol of the American Dream. Somewhere my "right" to life, liberty, and pursuit of happiness had crowded out my Lord's plans for me.

I put so much focus on acquiring a house, settling in, and living the American Dream that I felt cheated by our hard times, like God let me down. It took awhile to realize that the American Dream and God's will are not necessarily synonymous.

It felt good for God to take the throne of my heart. I was glad He'd allowed the pain in my life that fall. It was worth it to have such peace inside.

When the worship time at church turned to praise songs, I did something I'd never done before. I couldn't help it! My whole being had to show God how much I loved Him. I looked nervously around the room, trying to find a place of escape. I HAD to dance to Him—and I wasn't attending one of those churches where dancing was normal protocol!

With the music singing through my soul I slipped out of the sanctuary into the empty foyer. Hiding behind closed doors I raised my hands to the King—twirled in circles, knelt before Him. I ached to express my worship—for He was more truly my King than I'd ever understood.

How about you, my friend? Are there idols in your heart that get in the way of your freedom? Is there something so dear to you that it blocks God's working in your soul? Is it so precious you are afraid to surrender it?

I can't promise that letting go won't hurt, but I do know that a heart surrendered to God brings peace . . . and as you let go you just might learn to dance!

Precious King of Kings and Lord of Lords, I thank You for the cleansing of false gods You've already given my heart, and I give You permission to keep up this work for the rest of my life. Topple any idol that blocks my freedom and relationship with You. Be exalted, Lord! You alone deserve my worship.

Week Two ~ Joining the Dance
Day 5: Sparkling on the Dance Floor

Giver of life, creator of all that is lovely,
Teach me to sing the words to your song;
I want to feel the music of living
And not fear the sad songs
But from them make new songs
Composed of both laughter and tears.

Teach me to dance to the sounds of your world
And your people,
I want to move in rhythm with your plan,
Help me to try to follow your leading
To risk even falling
To rise and keep trying
Because you are leading the dance.
> *~ Author Unknown (Excerpt found in "You*
> *Gotta Keep Dancin'" by Tim Hansel)*

Before the sun came up I awoke to mounds of white
shimmering in the soft light cast by the lamp pole in front of
our home. As the sun rose I marveled at the fresh, clean

beauty. That night we went out. The road in front of our car danced with the sparkle of a thousand diamonds. Our headlights provided the music—illuminating the brilliance.

It seemed appropriate. I'd plodded through a barren fall that culminated in deep cleansing. Winter offered a purity symbolized by the white snow. When I returned home I crawled into my blue recliner, reached for my journal, and penned a new prayer.

I pray I am like the snow—shining and dancing as God pours His light of truth into my life. I'm afraid it is more likely I am shielding my eyes and that my feet are heavy and plodding. I should dance! The Master of the Universe is singling me out for this round!! He's asking like the old song, 'Can I have this dance for the rest of your life?'

I see Him in a gentlemanly fashion reaching His hand to me. One eyebrow is slightly raised in invitation. Will I join His dance? Will I let Him lead? Will I truly give myself to His music—His timing, rhythm, and beat—so that I can move as one with Him?

I want the light He shines into my life to illuminate me. I want others to see the new sparkle He brings into me—I want it to glisten and bounce right off me onto the people I love and the people I am yet to love.

Oh Jesus! That I may join You in the Light Dance! Help me to float effortlessly in Your arms, submitting gleefully to Your will— sparkling on the dance floor of life.

Awaken

Week Three ~ A Stumble in the Dance

Week Three ~ A Stumble in the Dance

Day 1: No Condemnation

There is therefore now no condemnation for those who are in Christ Jesus.
   ~ Romans 8:1 (NKJV)

I sat on the gray carpet of my bedroom floor staring at my open Bible. There was a stirring inside, like God was trying to tell me something, but I couldn't quite understand what it was. I flipped my Bible shut and walked away. The incident happened several years ago, but I've never forgotten it—that confused feeling of almost grasped truth.

   See, I had a real problem with guilt. When we first married, my husband often teased me. "What's wrong?" he'd ask, "Haven't you had your guilt trip yet today?" As I've matured I've come to understand that guilt controlled my life. I often did things that God hadn't called me to do because of my fear of guilt.

   I found myself constantly trying to please everyone so I wouldn't have to feel guilty about anything I'd said or done. On top of that, I couldn't feel consistently close to God. After all, how could I when I failed so often?

My loving Lord grew tired of it.

He was tired of watching me hurt as I lived without an understanding of the freedom of the cross. How He must have wearied of watching the enemy steal my joy! I think He was also done with my allowing others to control me.

I've no doubt it grieved God as I plodded through my days, head bowed in shame, heart weighted with failure. He wanted to hold me in His arms and lead me in the dance of life.

When I finally became miserable enough to cry out to Him for relief, He met me in my pain and showed me He'd taken all my condemnation.

Satan is given a variety of names in scripture, but the one I think is most revealing is The Accuser. It goes right along with another of his names, The Deceiver. Satan accuses me, makes me wallow in shame, and then deceives me into thinking God is shaking His finger at me in disgust.

Which leads to another of his names, The Thief—the one who steals the joy of my salvation. The one who robs me of experiencing the delight my Father feels for me. Jesus says, "The thief's purpose is to steal and kill and destroy. My purpose is to give life in all its fullness" (John 10:10, NLT).

How often in the old days I cowered before a loving God, crushed under the guilt of failing Him when all the while He had His arms around me, waiting for me to understand that I was completely forgiven, loved, and accepted. Satan blinded me to this glorious truth.

We all make mistakes in life—some so big that we are afraid to admit them. We think we couldn't handle the guilt if we did. But that's the point of the cross. Christ died to set us free from cycles of failure and shame.

Is there something in your life that leaves you so

consumed with guilt you can't let it go? Is guilt a daily companion, sneaking in every time you think you've disappointed someone or messed up?

Do you need to take Christ at His word?

He isn't standing there condemning you. When you invited Him to be your Lord, He took your guilty heart and replaced it with a new clean one.

His finger isn't wagging at you; it's underneath your chin, gently lifting your face to His so you can see the love in His eyes.

Precious Jesus! You took all my guilt and shame. Help me live in the freedom of one who is no longer condemned.

Week Three ~ A Stumble in the Dance
Day 2: Perfect Complete Acceptance

Who dares accuse us whom God has chosen for his own? Will
God? No! He is the one who has given us right standing with
himself. Who then will condemn us? Will Christ Jesus? No, for he
is the one who died for us and was raised to life for us and is
sitting at the place of highest honor next to God, pleading for us.
　　~ Romans 8:33–34 (NLT)

Have you ever felt raw, vulnerable, exposed? Like the facade
you thought was you got ripped away leaving a crumbled
mass of inadequacy? I have. It felt like a dagger piercing my
heart again and again. My sins lay bare before me, and all I
could do was grieve.

　　When Mel Gibson's *Passion of the Christ* opened, it
caused quite a stir. People were shocked by its portrayal of
the physical suffering of Jesus. The brave saw themselves as
the cause of Christ's pain. As horrific as His physical torture
was, I wonder if His spiritual agony was much worse.

　　The Bible says that Christ BECAME sin for us. I've
glimpsed the anguish of facing a piece of my own sinfulness.
What must it be like to BECOME sin—to take upon Oneself

the sin of not only every person in the world, but of every generation who has lived on this earth?

How did Jesus endure the utter defeat of sin—the complete rejection of His Father—as He hung on the cross, paying for my every fault?

I felt the dagger of my sin recently. I sat in bed, leaning into my husband's arms, sobbing as I grieved my sins. I awoke the next morning to this phrase from a popular praise song, "I'll never know how much it cost to see my sin upon the cross."

I thought perhaps I'd experienced a minuscule glimpse of my Lord's pain at Calvary. The funny thing is, Christ willingly received the grotesque, gut-wrenching grief of my sin so I don't have to.

Is it really true—this gift of forgiveness?

Does God really look at me (even as I sin) as His beloved, clean child?

When confronted with my own ugliness, my only choices are to live in my sin and shame or accept God's forgiveness. I don't deserve it. I can't earn His acceptance. I can only embrace the cross of Christ in passionate gratitude.

Only as I let the truth of His love sink in can I move forward.

In the dance of life I think we often stumble out of step with our Lord because of our inability to accept His grace. He's on the dance floor, wanting to waltz with us, hold us in His arms through our every failure, but we turn our head in shame, unable to receive the love and acceptance He offers.

The morning after I'd grieved my failures it hit me that my husband had been a picture of Christ to me the night before. My sins, many of which were against him, changed nothing between us. He just held me, let me grieve my faults, and accepted me.

Dear one, it's okay to face those sins you want to ignore. Let them lead you to the Father's arms. As you embrace Christ's sacrifice for you there is no condemnation—just perfect, complete acceptance.

Father, I accept Your unconditional forgiveness. I believe I am loved, accepted, and embraced by You. Thank You, Jesus, for taking my sin upon Yourself. Holy Spirit, teach me to live as I truly am. Forgiven.

Week Three ~ A Stumble in the Dance

Day 3: Jubilant Freedom

It is for freedom that Christ has set us free.
  ~ Galatians 5:1 (NIV)

"It is for freedom that Christ set you free." The snippet of Scripture, personalized just for me, repeated over and over, echoing in my mind as I awoke. I threw back my floral comforter and grabbed my Bible. I didn't even take time to find a chair, just sat on the floor, opened God's Word, and scanned the concordance for the reference of the rest of the verse.

"Stand firm, then, and do not let yourselves be burdened again by a yoke of slavery" (Galatians 5:1, NIV).

I understood then what the Spirit was saying. I had lived my life bound by guilt. Enslaved, I lived in bondage to condemnation and fear of failure! God had set me free. Now that I was beginning to grasp what that meant He didn't want me going backwards. He wanted me to live forever free!

Later the text says, "You who are trying to be justified by the law have been alienated from Christ; you have fallen away from grace" (Galatians 5:4, NIV).

I was learning, ever so slowly, that my efforts to be good enough prevented me from experiencing God's grace. These efforts kept me in a continuous cycle of pride and guilt—feeling good when I succeeded and wallowing in shame when I failed. Because I thought God demanded this from me I often couldn't find His love. I either had pride so I didn't know how much I needed Him or so much guilt I was ashamed to be with Him.

I'd accepted Jesus into my life so that I could be saved from hell and had promptly forgotten the cross. I thought He saved me and then spent the rest of my life frustrated with me when I sinned. Always watching to see if I got the Christian life right. Shaking His finger at me when I blew it.

How far from the truth that thinking was!

Because I tried so hard to follow the rules and be a good Christian, I never really grasped freedom. The Christian life was a tightrope walk, not a dance where I followed my loving Lord's lead. I didn't understand freedom because I still lived under the law. I strove, with all that was in me, to be good—to do what was right.

But for God I'd still be there.

Jesus not only did the freeing work of the cross, He sent His Holy Spirit to whisper to me, helping me understand that a life lived in grace could be free of all that guilt and striving.

Won't you join me in looking to Jesus and experiencing His love? Together we can walk away from the bondage of guilt and pride. Together we can rest in His promise to make us holy. Come! Relish with me the jubilant life of freedom!

Hallelujah, what a thought!
Jesus full salvation brought,
Victory, victory;
Let the pow'rs of sin assail,
Heaven's grace can never fail,
Victory, victory.

Victory, yes, victory.
Hallelujah! I am free,
Jesus gives me victory;
Glory, glory! hallelujah!
He is all in all to me.

I am trusting in the Lord,
I am standing on His Word,
Victory, victory;
I have peace and joy within,
Since my life is free from sin,
Victory, victory.

Shout your freedom everywhere,
His eternal peace declare,
Victory, victory,
Let us sing it here below,
In the face of every foe,
Victory, victory.
            ~Excerpts from "Victory" by Barney E Warren

Week Three ~ A Stumble in the Dance
Day 4: Let's Try It This Way

For God is greater than our worried hearts and knows more about us than we do ourselves.
  ~ I John 3:20 (MSG)

I threw my Bible across the room. "God!" I yelled, "How can you ask me to be completely patient when I often can't even be partially patient for fifteen minutes?"

I'd been studying Ephesians for weeks, enjoying the glorious truths of the first three chapters. But then I came to chapter 4, verse 2. "Be completely humble and gentle; be patient..." That word "completely" messed with the old me, the perfectionist. I could never be completely anything.

The Lord reminded me of the three chapters of Ephesians that preceded the verse that upset me. They spoke of how I was raised up with Christ and seated in the heavenly places, blessed with every spiritual blessing. They told me I was God's workmanship, the dwelling place of His Spirit, and that ALL He'd given me was a free gift, nothing I could earn.

The passage closest to the verse that upset me was

Paul's prayer that I would come to know the breadth, length, height, and depth of God's love so that I could be filled up to the fullness of God.

"Paula," the Lord whispered to my heart. "All your life you have tried to be good. Just focus on knowing Me and let *Me* make you good."

It was yet another paradigm shift as God moved me from a mindset of spiritual performance to one of walking in grace. In His goodness He came to me over and over, asking me to release guilt and shame into His loving hands. Teaching and reteaching me how to walk with Him in freedom.

A friend of mine had a dream that illustrated what the Lord showed me that day. In her dream she walked in a dense forest. Suddenly she tripped over a huge root and fell. She hadn't seen it sticking up in her path, but, ashamed of her misstep and subsequent fall, she cowered on the ground.

She expected God to reprimand her.

The Lord walked over to her and gently lifted her to her feet. "Let's try it this way," He said. His voice, gentle and compassionate, held no condemnation.

Instead of feeling guilty for failure and striving to be a good Christian, I am learning to live free. My only "job" is to focus on Jesus, getting to know Him better every day. The Father does the rest, remaking me to be more like His son (Romans 8:29). He lifts me to my feet when I fall and gently shows me a better way.

Your infinite patience heals me as You free me from a life of guilt and striving. Thank you. Teach me to accept Your outstretched hand when I stumble instead of cowering on the ground consumed with my faults.

Week Three ~ A Stumble in the Dance

Day 5: Hello Freedom!

Let us strip off every weight that slows us down, especially the sin that so easily trips us up. And let us run with endurance the race God has set before us. We do this by keeping our eyes on Jesus, the champion who initiates and perfects our faith.
~ Hebrews 12:1–2 (NLT)

It seemed the children had bickered all day. Each time I settled an argument the muscles in my neck twitched and the rock in the pit of my stomach grew heavier. A homeschooling mom, I have plenty of opportunity to interact with my children.

That day one of them exploded as I taught spelling, another argued with me over a reading lesson, and everyone seemed to forget their chores. By bedtime my shoulders slumped. I forced myself through their bedtime routine, praying prayers I didn't feel.

When the house was finally quiet, I wrote in my journal then turned out the light and put on my favorite CD. I lay on the couch, huddled under an afghan, totally defeated, mourning my sins of omission, listening to a singer who knew the grief of failure.

"After all," I told myself, "if I was a good mother my children wouldn't talk back, bicker, or be angry." Good mothers had better discipline. Good mothers had more patience. Good mothers had done a better job in the early years, and their post-preschool children would always be obedient and kind—and of course a good mother could go to bed with a clean kitchen because the children had done their chores without being reminded!

As I lay in the dark, I asked God to help me—to reveal His truth. It came a few days later as I sat in my blue recliner, writing a prayer in my journal. I discovered I had done it again! Taken guilt that wasn't mine. Blamed myself when Christ had declared me blameless . . . and what made it even worse is that I took my children's sins upon myself as well. (As though I didn't have enough of my own!)

The Lord showed me I had to release my children to Him. To let them be human. Like me, they weren't perfect. Like me, they needed to own their sins and let Him forgive.

How could they learn to follow their Lord in the dance of life if I stayed in the way, confusing them by blaming myself for their mistakes?

My children didn't need me as their savior. They already had One.

My children also didn't need a perfect mother who knew how to settle every argument, discipline away every stray word, and tame every rebellion.

They had a Lord for that.

They needed to confront their own need for the Holy Spirit's moment-by-moment intervention and empowerment.

Besides, if they had a perfect mother, how could they

ever understand life?

I'm beginning to understand how closely perfectionism and guilt are tied together. If the enemy can make me think I should be perfect he can quickly defeat me . . . and I'm back in that same old ugly cycle of guilt and failure.

Pretty smooth.

Perfectionism rears its ugly head too often in my life. It makes me angry when I don't accomplish my to-do list. It causes me tension when I step over clutter and embarrasses me when I find a misspelled word in something I've written. Perfectionism sets unreachable standards for myself and causes me to take on other people's faults.

I do know One who is perfect, though.

He's the Author and Perfecter of my life.

He's the One who takes all my mistakes, sins, inadequacies, and failures and weaves them into something beautiful and good.

He's the One who replaced my old, messy human heart with His own perfect one. Come to think of it, He's the One who set me free from striving so hard to be perfect! After all, through Jesus I am perfect—to God.

Where does perfectionism trap you? Maintaining the perfect body? Getting the best evaluation at work? Presenting a together image? Being the perfect student, parent, child, friend, spouse, . . . or Christian?

Let it go, my friend!

Thank goodness our Lord completed the job on the cross. We can quit striving to be good and rest in His work. It's a done deal.

The only perfect One is our Lord. He's the One who promises to transform us into the likeness of Himself.

Good-bye perfectionism! Good-bye guilt!
Hello Jesus!
Hello freedom!

Oh precious Jesus, my lover, forgiver, sustainer, and completer!
Thank You for a life free from guilt and shame!

Week Four ~ The Father's Parent Heart

Week Four ~ The Father's Parent Heart

Day 1: The Throne Room

Let us therefore come boldly to the throne of grace, that we may obtain mercy and find grace to help in time of need.
~ Hebrews 4:16 (NKJV)

I knelt in front of my blue recliner, petitioning the Lord while the house was quiet. "You said in Your Word that I could come boldly before the throne of grace so here I come."

"Where are you, Paula?" The Lord interrupted. "When you come before my throne?"

A piece of a Scripture flitted through my mind, something about being seated with Christ in the heavenlies.

"Sitting with Jesus?" I responded.

"And where is He?"

"At Your right hand?"

The prompting in my heart was quiet.

Grabbing my Bible I looked for the Scripture the Lord brought to mind. I found it in Ephesians 2:6. "And God raised us up with Christ and seated us with him in the heavenly realms in Christ Jesus" (NIV).

It became clear why the Lord stopped my prayer. I'd approached Him as though I didn't belong. "Claiming" Hebrews 4:16, I clung to it for the courage to make my requests. I saw myself, heart pounding, holding my little scrap of Scripture to gain entrance to presence of God.

It was as though I were an outsider, entering the throne room, marching down a long corridor lined with the heavenly host, and then demanding an audience.

My loving Father reminded me that I was His very *own*. I BELONGED in the throne room; I was seated right beside Him in Christ. I flipped to Hebrews 4:16 and wrote in the margin. "I approach His throne from my position of being seated with Christ in the heavenlies (Eph 2:6). I can approach God as one already close to Him."

God's word says I'm His child (John 1:12), adopted by the Father (Eph 1:5), and united with Him (1 Cor 6:17). Through Christ's death on the cross I've not only been given access to the royal room, I've become one of the family! In Ephesians 1:5 we're told that God, "predestined us to be adopted as his sons through Jesus Christ, in accordance with his pleasure and will" (NIV).

It *pleases* Him that we are His children!

That day my picture of prayer changed. No longer do I enter the throne room while trembling before the hosts of heaven. I'm more like a welcomed child, seated right next to my Daddy. When I need something, I just lean a bit to the left, and His arm envelops me.

Father, help me to feel Your arms around me when I come to You. Help me to remember I am always in Your Presence, right where my Loving Father desires me to be. Help me to truly believe I belong!

Week Four ~ The Father's Parent Heart

Day 2: God's Delight

He will take delight in you with gladness.
With his love, he will calm all your fears.
He will rejoice over you with joyful songs.
~ Zephaniah 3:17 (NLT)

Stephen's blue eyes were wide, and a solitary tear ran down his cheek. I quickly sat on the flannel sheets of his bed.

"What is it, honey?"

"I'm thinking about Grandpa and missing him."

My throat constricted as I hugged him. Then, I cupped his face in my hands and wiped the tear off his freckles with my thumb. "What made you think about that again?"

"The story you told about him yesterday. I've been thinking about it ever since."

"But that was a happy story, and it's been a long time since you've felt sad about Grandpa."

His little hand wrapped itself around my arm and he looked at me earnestly. "Just because the story is happy and he's been gone a while doesn't mean all the grief is gone out of my heart." He spoke with wisdom beyond his seven years.

I caressed his cheek, wiping another tear.

"Sometimes I wish he'd died before I was born so I wouldn't have to miss him so much, but," he added, "then I wouldn't have had all those happy times with him either."

I gazed down at him seeking for a way to ease his pain, praying silently. "You know, sweetheart," I finally said, "as good as the memories of Grandpa are, he gave you something even more special that will always be in your heart."

Stephen's eyes searched mine. His hand squeezed harder.

"Gramps showed you what it feels like when someone loves to be with you. He delighted in you, Stephen. Now your heart knows what it means to be special. Gramps showed you how God feels about you. For the rest of your life you can know deep inside how much God loves and enjoys you because Grandpa showed you."

Peace settled over his face, and he nuzzled his head against my arm. I thought about the truth in my words—words that surprised me even as I said them.

Memories often fade too quickly, and I can't remember the sights, smells, and colors of special moments, but what my loved ones gave me go deeper than memories.

Their love imprinted God's love upon my heart.

They showed me that someone delighted in me. Because of that experience I am able to open my heart to the truth that God delights in me.

When my children were little, my husband and I would often sit and watch them, enthralled by their little actions. Now that they are older we delight in them as they mature. We rejoice with them as they discover their unique personalities, skills, and passions.

We love simply being with them.

Sadly, many in the world have never known what it means to be delighted in, to understand they are special to someone important. Even those of us who've known delight can find it difficult to believe God delights in us as adults. Our failures and weaknesses prey upon us.

But the truth is, just as we find joy in our children simply because they are ours, so our Father delights in us just because we are His. We didn't earn His love, nor can we lose it. Zephaniah 3:17 says God will "take great delight in you, he will quiet you with his love, he will rejoice over you with singing" (NIV).

His delight never ceases.

Do you hear the whisper of His song?

Precious Father, quiet me with Your love. Tune my ears to hear Your singing. Open my heart to believe I am Your delight.

Week Four ~ The Father's Parent Heart
Day 3: The Right Medicine

Can a woman forget her nursing child, and have no compassion on the son of her womb? Even these may forget, but I will not forget you.
~ Isaiah 49:15 (NASB)

"I just need someone to hold me." Before me stood my firstborn son, Seth, cheeks flushed red with fever and glassy eyes full of need.

My fingers on the keyboard stopped mid-word. Seth, on the threshold of manhood, had broad shoulders and a strong, athletic body, which, along with passion and hours of practice, helped make him the "#1" ranked player in his hockey league. How many more opportunities would I have to soothe his hurts with the simple of act of holding?

"Meet me at the recliner," I said, leaving a sentence fragment behind a flashing cursor on my computer screen.

His buddies at the rink might have been shocked to see my highly competitive son curled up on my lap. I rocked him in our blue recliner, gently touching his fevered forehead. I held him close as his painful gulps slowed into peaceful breaths and the tense lines on his face disappeared.

"This helps me," he whispered.

A few days earlier my daughter had fought the same illness. A junior higher, Sarah was a real trooper, showing her maturity by keeping mostly to her room and resting while I continued our homeschool schedule with her brothers. As a little girl she wouldn't have endured such solitude, especially when sick.

As soon as I was more available, though, Sarah slipped into the living room where her dad and I sat. "I just need you to hold me," she implored, fighting the tears her swollen throat and aching body were bringing to the surface. Her dad got her some pain reliever, and I pulled her on my lap, snuggling her beneath her lavender comforter.

After awhile Sarah seemed to ease. "Is the medicine starting to help you, honey?" I asked.

She gave me a sweet, lopsided grin and whispered, "Which medicine? The Tylenol or you?"

Later, Sarah's dad took a turn. I watched, touched by her look of peace as she curled in his arms.

Seth stirred, bringing me back to the present. I pulled him closer, thankful my children asked us to hold them when they hurt, even as they matured.

My mind drifted to my own life—to the times I needed Someone bigger, stronger, and healthier to hold me. It didn't seem to matter how much I "grew up" or how life's lessons built my spiritual muscles, there was never a time I didn't need my Father holding me tight.

I learned to tell Him every detail, every emotion, every hurt—and to then sit quietly and accept His love. His Word said He promised to hold me as a mother held her weaned child. That kind of love I understood, the love of a parent who pulled you close even after your baby days were over.

"Thank you, Lord," I whispered. "It helps me."

I smiled. When the next unhealthy, painful time in life came, I'd know what to do—just reach for the right medicine and climb on up.

Thank You, Father, for loving me like a caring parent. You are the medicine my heart needs. Help me trust it is safe to curl up in Your arms.

Day 4: As a Mother Comforts Her Child

As a mother comforts her child, so will I comfort you.
~ Isaiah 66:13 (NIV)

"I figured it out."

Glancing in the rearview mirror I caught the very serious, yet pleased look on my four-year-old daughter's face. "What did you figure out, honey?"

Sarah's green eyes shone. "How God takes care of our baby." Pointing to my swollen tummy, her little hands gesturing and the bright pink rubber band on her ponytail bobbing, she explained, "See, He made stairs that go from your heart down to your tummy. When our baby cries, Jesus comes out of your heart, goes down those stairs, picks up the baby, and rocks him back to sleep." She ended with a triumphant smile on her face, then demonstrated by rocking her imaginary doll.

I nodded seriously with a noncommittal "Ahem" and hid the grin creeping across my face. It was one of many of Sarah's efforts to understand the big things in life—you know, things like how God can live inside of us, love us, and take care of our needs. Maybe her thoughts about staircases in tummies wouldn't thrill a theologian (or a scientist!), but I believe she glimpsed God's heart.

Sometimes God seems far away, but even at four Sarah understood that He never is—that, in fact, He dwells within us. She hadn't yet memorized the Bible verses, but she already understood the truth of Isaiah 66:13. She believed in God's mother heart, a heart that comforts us in our pain. She understood that God has a mother's ears, ears that hear the cries of His children.

It seems we hear more about God's father heart than His mother heart—but Scripture clearly shows He loves us as a mother does. There are verses that talk of how He wants to care for us as a mother cares for her nursing child or as a hen gathers her baby chicks under her wings.

The incident with my daughter happened years ago. Sarah doesn't see God as a tiny Jesus walking down stairways in my tummy anymore, but I can't help but believe even as a little girl she understood something many of us grown-ups miss. Sarah saw God's mother heart, understanding that when we cry He finds a way to hold us.

Father God, teach me to trust Your nurturing care. Reveal to me the ways You love as a mother who longs to comfort her child.

Week Four ~ The Father's Parent Heart

Day 5: When I Can't Feel His Love

God is love.
  ~ 1 John 4:8 (NIV)

Love is who God is. Loving is what God does.

For most of my early life I didn't get it. While I could quote the Scripture, "God is love" and sing the song, "Jesus loves me," I thought God pulled away from me when I failed.

I believed things like whether or not I'd prayed and read my Bible that day, whether or not I'd kept my spending within the budget, or whether or not I had control of my temper determined how God would respond to me.

The Christian life was about me and how well I did.

My times of peace were fleeting because I based my perception of God's love toward me upon my own actions. I disapproved of myself, so how could He approve?

I performed for Him, but when I didn't meet His standards I couldn't feel His love.

If God seemed far away I figured I wasn't trying hard enough.

I'm learning to live the truth: I am loved because God is love. He loves me like a good Father whose love never wavers, good days or bad.

Some of us had parents who modeled God's unconditional love. Some of us didn't. Many of us have both kinds of memories—times when our parent loved freely as well as times we felt rejected when we didn't please them.

But God doesn't love more when we succeed than when we fail. He doesn't give Himself to us because we're good enough.

He loves us because it is who He is.

He is incapable of anything less.

If we can't earn God's attention, if His love is ours no matter how we behave, what do we do with the fact He sometimes feels far away?

Like you, I've wrestled with this on more than one occasion. One time I went through a season where God felt very close. I woke up with love songs in the morning and truth leapt off of the pages of the Bible and jumped into my heart. Sometimes I'd spend two or three hours alone with Him and feel frustrated because it wasn't enough.

But then it all stopped.

I tried to spend time alone with God, but I overslept. When I did get up before the children to grab time for prayer and Bible reading, it felt dry. I couldn't make myself do the things or feel the things that happened so naturally just months before. An old slogan haunted me: "If God feels far away guess who moved?"

But I didn't feel like I moved.

I had teaching that if God felt far away it was because I'd sinned. I grappled with this. I wasn't living my life differently than when God felt near. Besides, that thinking went against everything He taught me in the season He'd felt so close. The Christian life was about Christ's performance at the cross, not my performance. I was close to my Father because Jesus did what it took to reconcile me to Him.

During this dry time, I experienced a series of particularly hard circumstances. I drove toward home one evening crying out, "I don't get it! Why do You seem close sometimes and other times so far away? I don't understand my suffering and struggles. I don't get why I can't feel or hear You right now. I don't know why I have to hurt so much."

And then, without even knowing they would be my next words, an epiphany fell from my lips. "I don't understand anything . . . except that I am completely accepted and loved by You.

"And it is enough."

And it was.

Sometimes I think about that epiphany when I round the same corner near my house. A lot has happened since then. Some of it was extremely difficult.

I didn't always feel happy with God or life while going through trials, but this understanding got me through: No matter the circumstances, no matter my success or failure, God loves me.

He loves you, too.

Always. Deeply. Completely.

And we have hope because HIS love does not disappoint us.

It is constant.

It is true.

He is our Father of unconditional love.

And it is enough.

Dear God, don't let me forget that when You look at me You love me. Keep me from doubting Your love when times are difficult or You seem far away. Help me to believe You are the kind of Father whose love is never conditional. Help me to know Your love is enough.

Awaken

Week Five ~ Jesus Our Lover

Week Five ~ Jesus Our Lover

Day 1: He Thought of Me

For the Lord your God has arrived to live among you. He is a mighty Savior. He will give you victory. He will rejoice over you in great gladness; he will love you and not accuse you. Is that a joyous choir I hear? No, it is the Lord himself exulting over you in happy song.
> ~ *Zephaniah 3:17–18 (TLB)*

Picturing Christ on the cross I was deeply moved as the congregation sang, "Crucified, laid behind a stone, You lived to die rejected and alone, like a rose trampled on the ground, You took the fall . . ."

I envisioned my Lord on the cross, pictured His arms outstretched, His head dipping in agony. Christ taking my sin.

"… And thought of me, above all …"*

Suddenly the picture in my mind changed, growing beyond my pondering.

Christ stood before me.

I watched as though a movie played before me.

Jesus reached for my hands, and we twirled in a

happy circle. As we danced He threw back His head and laughed in sheer joy.

I sensed His heart though I heard no words. "This is why I did it," he said, "to enjoy you forever."

Enjoy me?

A thrill ran through me, and I felt deeply loved. It seemed beyond comprehension that Jesus, King of Kings and Lord of Lords, enjoyed me so much He chose the cross so we could be together forever. Beyond comprehension, but oh so wonderful!

Zephaniah 3:17 says God thinks we're so special He actually sings over us. I once heard that a Jewish rabbi said, properly translated, the Scripture actually means He dances over us!

Take a moment. Can you see it? The God of the universe dancing with joy over you and me! Maybe initially the Three of them hold hands and form a circle, dancing around us. Then perhaps the Persons of the Trinity take turns. Jesus, the bridegroom, pulls us close to one of those slow, romantic melodies. God the Father chooses a sentimental song for the Father-daughter dance, and on-lookers wipe their eyes. Then the party gets going, and Holy Spirit calls us up to teach us a new line dance.

Maybe my imagination is carrying me away, but these images bring home to me the Scriptures that call Jesus the groom and me His bride. Coupled with the image I received that day in church it is easier to believe Jesus chose the cross not only out of obedience to His Father, but because He looked forward to His inheritance, the wedding gift His Father promised—you and me.

Jesus, help me to truly believe You enjoy me. Rejoice over me.

Delight in me. Want to dance with me. Thank You for Your bridegroom love. Open my heart to receive it in ever-increasing measure.

* "Above all" by Lenny LeBlanc and Paul Baloche

Week Five ~ Jesus Our Lover

Day 2: As the Bridegroom Rejoices

As a bridegroom rejoices over his bride, so will your God rejoice over you.
  ~ Isaiah 62:5 (NIV)

I didn't know before class that a thirteen-year-old would usher me further into God's heart. We sat on hard gray folding chairs lining old brown tables and dreamed of a place much more beautiful. We talked about the things we anticipated most in eternity—seeing Christ for the first time, exploring the home He'd prepared for us, seeing loved ones we missed.

"Miss Paula," Jennie spoke in her soft, gentle voice, "when I think about the first time I'll see Jesus, I picture myself in a flowing white dress. I'm standing in a forest full of flowers, and there's a beautiful river nearby. I look up and see Him running toward me. I mean, I want to run to Him, but He's running to me! He's wearing a crown, and in His hands He carries another, for me."

Stunned, I was captured by her words—glimpsing a piece of God's heart I hadn't seen before. In the Bible God calls us His bride, but I had never seen myself in a white dress, and I'd always thought I should go to Him, never considering He might run to me!

As I've pondered her words I'm drawn to a couple of Scriptures. The first, found in Isaiah 61:10, helps me see myself as that beautiful maiden in the forest. "I delight greatly in the LORD; my soul rejoices in my God. For he has clothed me with garments of salvation and arrayed me in a robe of righteousness, as a bridegroom adorns his head like a priest, and as a bride adorns herself with her jewels" (NIV).

As I read these words I begin to believe that God has indeed prepared me as a bride for Christ—that in His plan to be united with me He has covered me in His righteousness and made me beautiful.

Isaiah 62:5 convinces me that God might actually run toward me as my young friend pictured. "As a bridegroom rejoices over his bride, so will your God rejoice over you." In this scripture I glimpse God's desire to be with me. I can see Him running through the forest, His arms outstretched.

I can't fully grasp the many facets of God's love. In His word, among other things, I'm called His lamb, His servant, His child, a saint, His friend, His lover, and His bride.

It's easier to accept being a lamb—a lamb is so needy.

And a servant? Well, of course, working for God makes sense to my human pride.

A child? Sure. A child needs to be taken care of, and I know I do!

A saint? I don't feel like one most of the time, but I can take that on faith. Christ's blood has made me holy in God's eyes, right?

A friend? That starts to get tricky. A friendship seems so reciprocal.

But a lover and a bride?

That takes this thing to a whole new level!

How can the perfect, Holy One of the universe love ME like THAT?

God wants an intimate relationship with me. Everything He's done, from creation until now, has been done so we could be close.

He LOVES me. He WANTS to walk with me as He walked with Adam and Eve in the garden. He WANTS to listen to me and share my whole life. He WANTS to hold me close. He REJOICES over me. Oh! To fully grasp this love!

Precious Jesus, my Bridegroom and Lover, open my heart to Your boundless love. Peel away my doubts and keep me in an endless discovery of relationship with You.

Week Five ~ Jesus Our Lover

Day 3: Flowers from Jesus

For we know how dearly God loves us, and we feel this warm love everywhere within us because God has given us the Holy Spirit to fill our hearts with his love.
     ~ Romans 5:5 (TLB)

Early summer in northeastern Oklahoma meant thick green grass, branching tree limbs of large, full leaves, and flowers of all colors, but in 1987 all I saw looked dull gray. Hopelessness wiped the color from my life, and I watched it as if on an old black and white TV.

I wrote a poem called "The Pit" and wondered how I would ever climb out. My growing sense of despair kept me from the sunlight; holding me down with cold, muddy fingers in a hole, lonely and dark. Sometimes I thought about taking my own life.

Summer school was in full swing, and I walked to class disgusted with myself. I'd let my depression overwhelm me to the point I hadn't studied for an important test. After three years of working hard to maintain a high GPA, I feared this summer would blow it. I don't know why

I took a different route to my class that day. I just felt nudged out off my normal path. I followed the concrete road between two buildings. As I turned the corner, a brilliant splash of my favorite color broke through the black and white screen and burst into my gray heart.

I don't remember what kind of flowers they were. I just remember that the bush was full of them, and they were exactly that color of deep pink, not quite magenta, that I loved best.

It's the first time I remember receiving a bouquet from God.

No one will ever convince me the moment was a coincidence. It was a gift, pure and simple, and the sheer beauty of it helped me hang on a little longer.

Back then I hadn't thought of Jesus as my Bridegroom, but as I relive the experience it is easy to see how He romanced me. Like a fiancé who knew me well, He chose the perfect flowers to awaken my heart to joy. He offered His attention, and His notice of me lifted my weary heart.

Since that time, I've received other bouquets. One particularly trying winter a single bright yellow pansy bloomed the entire season. Its cheerful face peeked out at me from beneath the barren winter branches of the tree in front of my house. Its happy color waved at me as it looked over the top of light snowfalls or popped back up at me when a heavy snow melted. I'd walk to my front door with a weary heart, but as I put my key into the lock the pansy's joyful color exclaimed, "Have hope! God is near!"

Paul writes in Romans 5:3–5, "We can rejoice, too, when we run into problems and trials, for we know that they are good for us—they help us learn to be patient. And patience develops strength of character in us and helps us trust God more each time we use it until finally our hope and faith are strong and steady. Then, when that happens, we are able to hold our heads high no matter what happens and know that all is well, for we know how dearly God loves us, and we feel this warm love everywhere within us because God has given us the Holy Spirit to fill our hearts with his love" (TLB).

I studied these verses back in 1987, that dreadful year when I contemplated suicide. What I learned is if I believe in God I can live in hope instead of despair. Suffering is part of any life, but as I walk through trials there is one thing that undergirds me: the conviction I am loved.

Oh, Jesus! Lover of my soul! Help me live in the hope Your love gives. Remind me in the dreary gray days, that the flower of Your love blooms in my heart.

Week Five ~ Jesus Our Lover

Day 4: Longer Than

For he chose us in him before the creation of the world.
~ Ephesians 1:4 (NIV)

"It's hard for us to believe this, to really accept it," said my pastor, "but God is crazily, insanely, madly in love with us." The lights dimmed and candles about the room created a gentle ambiance. As he led us into worship, I pondered his words.

It was good to be reminded of the truth that God not only loved me, but was crazy *in love* with me. The Lord took me through a season where He revealed love for me in warm, romantic ways—gifts of flowers, words of Scripture that leapt from the page, and love songs in the morning.

My favorite memory from this period happened one crisp fall morning. I snuggled underneath my covers, not yet awake. As consciousness slowly overcame the cobwebs of slumber, I heard sweet music ringing in my heart.

The old song* filled my soul, "Longer than there've been fishes in the ocean, higher than any bird ever flew, Longer than there've been stars up in the heavens, I've been in love with you. I am in love with you."

The moment was so palpable, so tender, I knew my Lord sang to me of His love.

In *The Sacred Romance*, written by John Eldgredge and Brent Curtis, they talk about how God speaks His love to the world in a million different ways. They say the whole of history is the story of God's effort to romance our hearts and reveal His love to mankind. One of their many examples is the song God sang over me. They conclude it is a love song from our Creator to us, and whether the composer intended it or not, God's heart sang out each time that song filled the airways.

As I studied the words I had to agree. Could anyone else have loved before fish swam in the ocean or stars glittered in the sky? Could anyone but God understand a love higher than a bird can fly?

I'll never forget the swell of my heart that morning as I felt Him singing to me—but I have to admit that in the midst of that wonderful moment, I was petty. "But God," I whispered. "You love everyone like that, not just me."

I wanted that intimate moment to be just ours. I longed to be particularly special to Him, not just one of many He loved.

He whispered, "But you are uniquely special to me, Paula. I am so big that each of my beloved fits perfectly with a piece of my personality that no one else completes."

I lay still in my bed, awed there was a piece of God that related just to me. It reminded me of when Jerry, my husband, said I completed him. Jerry was fully himself before he married me, but something in our connection brought a sense of completion. I'm not surprised that Jesus would relate to me with this image of intimacy.

Have you received this truth into your heart—that there is a special relationship between you and God that no one else can share?

If not, I challenge you to ask Him to open your heart to the ways He calls to you in the sacred romance of your life.

Oh Lord! Let me hear Your love song whispered into the depths of my heart. Give me the faith to accept such an unfathomable love so that I can live in ever-deepening intimacy with You.

Note: This Scripture, as well as others I used in this week's devotions, was prophesied to Israel thousands of years ago. Because the New Testament says we are "grafted" into Israel, who are God's chosen people, I am comfortable receiving beautiful declarations like this as my own.

"Longer Than" by Dan Fogelberg

Day 5: Passionate Love

With unfailing love I have drawn you to myself.
  ~ Jeremiah 31:3 (NLT)
Expect love, love, and more love!
  ~ Jeremiah 31:3 (MSG)

There's something about the passionate love of a man for a woman. My favorite scene in the A&E miniseries *Pride and Prejudice* is when Mr. Darcy, trying to overcome his feelings for Elizabeth, dives into a pond, fancy clothes and all. My heart always beats a little faster at the intensity of Darcy's love illustrated by the emotion of that moment—the whoosh of the water followed by the eerie quiet underneath.

    I have a friend who couldn't watch that movie. It would set her back for days—longing to be truly, deeply, and romantically loved. She and her husband worked hard to overcome setbacks in their marriage and stuck with it through difficult times. Both of them grieved things from their past—things that make it tough for them to show each other the love they feel. Neither of them had healthy role models for marriage. Both entered the relationship with holes in their heart, hoping to find someone who could fill them.

For my friend, watching *Pride and Prejudice* was just another assault on her heart, a reminder of the love that seemed to elude her husband and her—until one day when she worked at her in-home business while her daughter watched the movie. My friend wanted to escape, but the TV and the workroom were in the same place.

Then the Lord broke through.

"I love you like that," He whispered to her heart.

In that moment the Lord destroyed the lie that my friend would never be truly loved.

Now she lives in the reality of love bigger than she'd ever imagined—the only love that can truly fill the holes in her heart. Now, when her husband is unable to meet her needs, she rests in the truth that she is always loved. Her newfound security has enabled her relate to her husband better as well. Since she's learning to let God fill the empty hole in her heart, she's able to see her husband's needs with new eyes and receive the love he *is* able to offer.

Years ago a different friend and I had a girls' weekend and went to a movie that affected me deeply. I remember saying to her, "Is real life ever that romantic?" When I returned home, I begged my husband to watch the movie with me. He wasn't interested. He'd read a review somewhere that it was based on romantic fluff and had no substance.

Recently my husband and I finally watched the movie together. It didn't affect me the same way, but being a little further along on my journey with the Ultimate Lover, I saw why I'd liked it so much.

The heroine in the story was a picture of Christ. She

loved the man in the movie selflessly with no expectation of return. While she saw his many faults, she also saw beyond them to the wounded man inside who needed someone to see the "real" him and offer a second chance. Though it made no sense, she fell deeply in love with him and gave him her life savings, never expecting to see it again.

That's true romance, isn't it? To be loved so passionately that we're desired by our Lover in our worst moments, not just our best? Real love sees past our wounds to the person we are meant to be. When we're loved like this, we can begin to turn from our ugliness and become the person our Lover sees, even when we have nothing to give in return, even when we don't deserve it.

That's the love of Jesus.

Jesus emptied Himself of the glory of heaven and gave His life so we could understand the passionate love He has for us. He died so He could love us for eternity. He loves us deeper and more romantically than every sappy movie we've ever seen.

He loves us with the passion of real love.

I can't describe the way God will fill the holes in your heart. Each of us has different needs and unique things that minister to us. In previous devotionals I told you how Jesus has loved me through songs and touches of beauty. My purpose in this week's devotions is not to describe how God will be your Lover, but rather to stir our hunger for Jesus our Lover.

Like any good marriage our relationship with Jesus is always growing and deepening and stretching. Maybe you've long walked with Jesus as Your Lover. Or maybe He's been your Husband but you've not quite seen Him as your Lover. A few years ago I hadn't even considered Jesus in this way. A deep study of the Song of Solomon along with other resources changed all that.

Whatever place you are in with Jesus, I encourage you to ask Him to reveal Himself to you in new ways. Let Him show you the holes in your heart and how He wants to fill them.

For me discovering Jesus as Lover wasn't an overnight event. There was a lot of learning about relationship with Him before I was able to receive His lover heart. Once I did there were plenty of days I struggled to believe in it, clinging to Scripture to help me. I'm comforted this concept is no longer hard for me to accept, but even as I can embrace this truth, I hunger to experience it more fully—and to grow in my ability to love Him back.

After all, Jesus is the best Lover of my soul. There is none like Him.

Jesus, my Lover, open my heart to Your complete, intense, and adoring love. Show me how to receive it and let it fill the holes in my heart. Then help me to passionately love you back.

Awaken

Week Six ~ Empowered by the Spirit

Week Six ~ Empowered by the Spirit

Day 1: Dependency

Know this: God, your God, is God indeed, a God you can depend upon. He keeps his covenant of loyal love with those who love him.
~ Deuteronomy 7:9 (MSG)

I finally get it.

I can't be who I want to be by my own effort. I can't make the personal changes I need to make, pursue the goals burning in my heart, or do anything of eternal significance without the power of the Holy Spirit.

When this truth was first settling deeply within, I prayed in earnest (for months!) that God would make me totally dependent on Him.

Ouch!

You probably guessed where this is going. I ended up in an ever-growing pile of circumstances beyond my control. God did a lot of pruning that season, cutting away things and people I had relied upon. But I learned a lot about depending on Him!

God is kind. Before He took me through the thick of the pruning, He gave me a gift. During one of the first intense weeks I got a card in the mail from a friend. It had a bookmark in it that my friend said she couldn't resist buying because it fit me so well.

The bookmark had my name on it and a meaning for Paula I'd never seen before: dependent on God.

Wow.

According to this definition my name meant the very thing I'd prayed I would become.

The only meanings for Paula I'd heard before were "small" and "little one." I didn't like those definitions. I'm tall for a woman, almost 5 foot 9 inches, and being the oldest child I rarely felt like a "little one." I was always told I was mature for my age, etc. etc.

When I received the card, I spent a lot of time praying and journaling to understand what God was saying. He showed me that most of my life He'd been training me to crawl up on His lap. When things happened that I couldn't handle, the Lord held and comforted me. I had always been *His* little one, even when I felt like an overly responsible oldest child. Even when I dealt with situations beyond the scope of a child's ability to handle.

I love my name now.

I love being God's little one, totally dependent on Him. It is my identity.

But I don't think this identity is only for people named Paula! Dependency on Him is God's heart for each of his children. As long as we look to anything but our God to undergird our lives, we depend on something less than perfect.

It's through abiding in God we discover all we are and can be. He is the only One trustworthy enough for complete dependence.

Holy Spirit, Help me rely on You for my strength, healing, and adequacy. Teach me to depend on You, not my own meager resources. Reveal Your loving faithfulness as I lean hard.

Week Six ~ Empowered by the Spirit

Day 2: Adequacy

And I will ask the Father, and He will give you another Helper
(Comforter, Advocate, Intercessor — Counselor, Strengthener,
Standby), to be with you forever.
    ~ John 14:16 (AMP)
At that moment you will know absolutely that I'm in my Father,
and you're in me, and I'm in you.
    ~ John 14:20 (MSG)

Paralyzed by fear, I stared at the blank screen. I was totally
inadequate to make the chapter "good enough." A new
fiction writer, I was out of my league. I'd poured over the
professional comments I received, read recommended works
on writing, done everything I knew to equip myself for the
task before me. Still, I didn't know how to do it!

It wasn't the first time I felt this way, and I'm sure it
won't be the last!

I've often felt incompetent. Homeschooling is a prime
example. It can leave me feeling like I'm trying to fill a tub of
water with a teaspoon. The job looms before me, calling for
patience, organization, skill, and time I know I don't have.

Emotional struggles or relational issues can also make me feel inept. I simply don't think I have the personal reserves to handle them. I'm not strong enough, wise enough, or brave enough to face them.

Ever so slowly I'm learning that I don't have to be adequate. Really!

And neither do you.

Dwight Edwards, in his wonderful book, *Revolution Within*, says, "My inadequacies aren't all there is to me. Within me there resides God's very nature of love, compassion, boldness, and wisdom and this is actually more central to who I am than any of my shortcomings."

Wow! *God* resides in *me*. And with Him all of *His* resources.

The core of who I am is who He is. I have immediate access to the power of the Creator of the Universe. He can teach when I cannot. He can write when I cannot. He can love when I cannot. ANYTHING I feel insufficient to tackle, He can handle!

As I've learned this truth I've taken baby steps of bravery—and a few giant ones! Starting a devotional website in 2004 was a leap. I didn't feel good enough, spiritual enough, talented enough, or disciplined enough to pull it off. God showed me that He already knew I wasn't up to the job. And since I finally admitted it, He had something to work with!

Thankfully, God is patient with me. I still hit walls of stifling fear. Life has a way of upping the stakes. When we overcome one challenge, a bigger one often presents itself! Sometimes my lack overwhelms me, and I cower. It doesn't seem to surprise Him when I go through these times. He just patiently reminds me that I don't have to be adequate because He is. As the old saying goes, "God and I are always a majority."

My every deficit is covered by His surplus.

Holy Spirit, I'm grateful that You are in me and we are one in God. Thank You for advocating for me, for teaching me what I don't yet understand, for comforting me in my fears. Empower me to be and do all I was created to be and do.

Week Six ~ Empowered by the Spirit

Day 3: Guidance

For we are God's workmanship, created in Christ Jesus to do good works, which God prepared in advance for us to do.
~ Ephesians 2:10 (NIV)

The other night I tossed and turned until close to midnight. I had a "to-do" list that felt longer than the Nile River and twice as deep. I finally climbed out of bed and worked until almost 4 a.m. The next day wasn't nearly so stressful thanks to those four hours of hard work with no interruption, but I'm still sleepy, days later.

What bothers me is not the fact that I had an especially full week, but wondering if the things I poured myself into will have lasting value. Am I listening to the Lord as I choose where to put my time?

Sometimes every need I hear of feels like a personal call to action. Pulled in a million directions, I struggle with where to put my time and energy.

In my efforts to trust God as I serve Him I've clung to scriptures like Philippians 4:13 which says that Christ will give me strength to do all things and 2 Timothy 3:17 that says God will equip me for every good work. While the Lord promises to give us strength and ability for the work He wants us to do, there is a danger in focusing on these thoughts without balancing them with Jesus' own example of taking time for rest and renewal.

Jesus often took time for himself, going to a quiet place to pray. He also enjoyed time with friends, eating in their homes and just hanging out with the ones He loved. Scripture shows Him seeking the Father's direction on when and how to tackle each task.

A good friend once told me, "The need is not the call." Yet, often I find myself chasing after more needs than I can keep up with, my stress level mounting, and my joy draining away, drip by drip, as I give without wisdom.

My dad used to tell me, "All work and no play makes Paula a dull girl." I chuckle a little at the memory of the old cliché, but recognize the voice of my Father in it as well. I don't believe our Creator shaped the splendor of a night sky, the delicate beauty of a flower, or the delighted smile of a child so that we would work without taking time to enjoy them.

Beyond that, I want my work to have eternal significance. I can dive into good works with the greatest intention, give to the point of exhaustion, and still not do anything that will have value for eternity. I don't want to spin my wheels doing things that don't really matter.

Sometimes a big assignment seems like the most important choice, but then the Lord redirects me to focus on family or inner peace. Other times He calls me into that task.

It's only through the guidance of His Holy Spirit that I know which call to answer. Ephesians 2:10 tells me I am God's own workmanship, created for His purposes and that

He has work He planned, long ago, for me to do. That's the work I want to be about.

Holy Spirit, as I gain confidence in Your ability to equip me for every good work, attune my ears to Your sweet guiding whisper. I want to choose those tasks that will have lasting value, those You prepared in advance for me to do, and I want to be wise enough to rest and renew when that is the best choice.

Week Six ~ Empowered by the Spirit

Day 4: Teacher

But the Helper, the Holy Spirit, whom the Father will send in My name, He will teach you all things.
  ~ John 14:26 (NKJV)

If I'd known how much I had to learn, I may never have started my first novel. But, full of naiveté, I plunged into the process, asking the Holy Spirit to lead me.

The first draft was so fun to write. I couldn't wait to get to my computer to see what would happen next. I laughed (and sometimes cried) as I typed away causing my husband to shake his head. One time he caught me crying and rushed to me in concern. Then, "Are you crying about what you just wrote?"

"Yes." I sniffed. "I didn't know the little boy would get hurt."

He moaned. "I may not survive your writing this book!"

I wrote that draft during every spare minute I could find. My husband graciously took all four children to baseball practices that summer, giving me precious moments alone with my book.

Concerned it might become an idol to me, I knelt at the couch during one of those alone times and asked the Lord if I should be talking with Him or reading my Bible instead of rushing to the computer. I felt Him whisper to my heart, "I thought we were writing this book together." Joyful, I turned on my CPU.

I finished my first draft, all 130,000 words, and bravely attended my first writer's workshop where I learned a whole list of things needed to improve my book. Excited, I went right to work and applied what I'd learned. During that second draft there were incredible moments of inspiration when I felt the Holy Spirit combine my life and my writing, whispering His truth into my novel.

Months later, a second draft complete, I attended another seminar. I learned some technical things I'd done wrong in my book and called my husband weeping. I'd have to rewrite the whole book to fix the problems.

After the initial emotion, I felt encouraged. I saw how the Holy Spirit taught me, inch by inch, exactly what I needed to know for each step of the process. If I'd been given all the teaching in one big lump the task would have been too overwhelming. I went back to the drawing board and began again.

Incrementally, the learning continued. Another teacher helped me find my own style. A book pointed out the mistakes that made me look like a beginner. A professional came alongside me when I lost heart, helped me contact editors and pointed out ways to improve my book and proposal. At a conference a famous author took a red pen to my first chapter, showing me little things, nuances and pacing, that improved my story. And the rewriting continues.

I've told the Lord I will walk through whatever doors He opens, that I want my writing to bring glory to Him and serve others. And so I ask Him to teach me.

I desperately want to see my book published: to feel the bound copy in my hands, smell the new book aroma, and share it with others. But even if it never sees publication I wouldn't trade the lessons I've learned for anything.*

I've discovered the Holy Spirit as my Teacher. For the last three years He has led every step of my writing journey. I've felt Him stir my heart as words pour onto a page, and I can catalog His tutelage—how He's led me to just the right person at the right time to learn what I was ready to learn. He never sent new information before I could receive it. But He always gave it just in time.

Only God can do that.

When Jesus prepared His disciples for His return to heaven, He told them He had to leave so the Holy Spirit could be given them. He promised His Spirit to all who believe upon His name. That's me. And you.

The Holy Spirit doesn't only help with the big tasks, like writing a novel. He leads and empowers us for every good work. Sometimes simply tackling the family's laundry and fixing a square meal seems overwhelming. And the Spirit is there.

I've prayed about what to fix for dinner more times that I can count. I've asked Him where I put my keys. I've given Him permission to probe those places inside that need His truth and healing.

He is always up to the task, big or small. And the best part is HE *lives* in ME! Within me (and you) reside the very mind, heart, and Spirit of God. If that's not enough resources to move forward, I don't know what is.

Holy Spirit, I need You. Thank You for helping me, teaching me in just the right way at just the right time. I want to surrender to Your tutelage."

*This devotion was initially written several years ago. I now have published novels available with more to come. Holy Spirit is indeed a wonderful Teacher!

Week Six ~ Empowered by the Spirit

Day 5: Comforter

And I will pray the Father, and he shall give you another
Comforter, that he may abide with you forever.
~ John 14:16 (KJV)

As the rough times pounded me, I curled (emotionally), tighter and tighter, into a fetal position.

All that week snippets of songs and scriptures about shelter and protection had found their way into my mind. One particular song had awakened me for several mornings in a row.

"You're my shelter through it all. You're my refuge and my strength. Lord, I hide in the shadow of Your wings." This song* had been His gift to me during one of the hardest, most frightening experiences of my life.

Why was He giving it to me again? Was I soon facing another assault? Fear grew.

Or maybe it was just uncovered.

That weekend I couldn't sit through the church service. The gnawing fear overwhelmed me. I slipped outside of the main room seeking privacy. I found a dark, empty classroom and curled up on the floor in that fetal position I'd felt all week.

As I lay there I imagined Aslan, the Lion who is the Christ prototype in C. S. Lewis's *The Lion, The Witch and the Wardrobe*, standing guard over me. I told the Lord I needed to hide there between Aslan's powerful paws, underneath his massive jaw.

Crying, I told the Lord everything I was afraid of, all the things I had tried to shove away and ignore. Some fears were almost silly. Others were deep, private, and penetrating, like a black hole with no light.

I saw myself, still in fetal position, leaning against one of Aslan's strong legs. As I continued to pray, protected on all sides by my imaginary Jesus Lion, I began to unfurl and sat on my bottom with legs in clasped hands and head resting upon my knees, thinking and seeking Him. Then I felt His massive head gently upon mine, like when I lean against my husband's chest and he lightly places his chin on my hair. It's a safe, tender place to be.

Before I finished praying I knew Aslan wanted me to walk forward with courage. But He didn't ask me to do it alone. As I moved ahead, He promised He would stand as I did. When I walked, He would walk. I'd fit there surrounded by his muscular front legs, underneath his powerful, tooth filled jaw. I could go in the same protection I sought when curled in that fetal position hiding from the fear.

Courage flowed; fears faded. I would walk. Soon.
But not that day.

Tired, I needed to sleep curled between His feet. Thankfully, I didn't have to do it in that tense, tightly squeezed ball. I placed my head upon His soft paw and draped my arm around His furry leg.

I slumbered in a field of flowers whose fragrance tended the wounds of my heart. I dreamed of awaking, climbing onto Aslan's back, running my fingers into his free flowing mane, and asking Him if he'd please run through the field with me. I thought maybe we could bound over a creek and splash underneath a waterfall. He understood that I needed to rest and play before I could stand and walk forward.

In John 14:16, Jesus promises us a Helper who will be with us forever. The *King James Bible* calls Him a Comforter, the *New International Version* calls Him an Advocate, and in *The Message* He is called Friend.

Our God, expressed as the Spirit who lives in us, meets us in whatever state our heart is in—even if it's the fetal position of fear. He comforts us, counsels us, and helps us walk forward. Like the lion, He dwarfs us with His sheer power and mass, yet, like Aslan, He is also completely committed to our well-being. He will take care of us forever.

He always knows just what we need.

Thank you, Holy Spirit, for dwelling in me. I trust You as my comforter and depend upon Your counsel. Remind me that Your power is always within my heart, and I am never alone.

*"Shadow of Your Wings," by Hillsong United

Awaken

Week Seven ~ God's Provision

Week Seven ~ God's Provision

Day 1: My Kitchen Table

So he built an altar there to the LORD, who had appeared to Him.
~ Genesis 12:7 (NIV)

Sometimes I forget the promise I made to remember God's care and trust Him for provision.

Our family went through a lean time. A business deal fell through, and with it crashed my dreams for repairs and upgrades in our home. I complained to a friend of mine who gently reprimanded me. "It sounds like you were trusting in that situation and not in the Lord to provide for your needs."

I wasn't so worried about my basic needs. I struggled to let go of my wants, especially my desire to replace a kitchen table and chairs that kept breaking and was duct-taped together. My friend had an answer for that as well. She told me about a time when she'd had a bad attitude and how she eventually looked to the Lord for furniture she needed. She found just what she wanted at a garage sale. It was exactly her taste and style, not just functional, but beautiful.

I knew God met my needs but hadn't dared believe He cared about my style and taste. That day I told the Lord I wouldn't be mad at Him if He didn't give me my desire, but I needed a new kitchen table, and I wanted the kind with a white tiled top and light blond wood. I hoped for four matching chairs and a bench to go across one side.

"If you give me one," I prayed, "it will be like an altar in my kitchen, reminding me You care about my tastes and desires. When I have hard times, I will look at the table, remember Your care, and trust You for provision."

Shortly after that my husband and I agreed on an amount I could spend if I found a second-hand table. I happened upon a big neighborhood sale. It was such a great find I called a friend who also liked bargain hunting and suggested she join us, which she did.

We found a kitchen set. It wasn't my favorite style, but it was solid wood and the right price. My friend, a talented seamstress, suggested ways to remake the chair cushions to fit my décor. As we studied it the owner interrupted us. The table had already sold.

Frustrated, I walked away. Sure it wasn't my dream table, but it was better than what I had. When I told my friend how much I wanted a new kitchen set, especially one with blond wood and white tiles, she looked at me kind-of funny. She had a white-tiled table and four chairs that were in her way. They had never been her style, and she no longer used them. Did I want them? When my husband found out she gave the set to me, he sent me to the nearest furniture store for a matching bench with money we'd set aside for a used table.

That table sat in my kitchen for years, a reminder of God's care for my needs *and* desires. I didn't always focus on

God's provision when I looked at it. I went about my business—served meals on it, wiped it off, and mopped under it—without a thought.

But always the table added cheer to the room and to my heart. The white top made me happy. My little girl often cut roses from our bush, and they looked so pretty adorning it. I loved to fill that table with good food and then sit around it and visit with loved ones. It blessed me even when I forgot to say thank you, an altar—like the stones the Israelites piled to remind them of God's great work in their midst.

In Matthew 5:25–26 Jesus says, "Do not worry about your life, what you will eat or drink; or your body, what you will wear . . . Look at the birds of the air; they do not sow or reap or store away in barns, and yet your Heavenly Father feeds them. Are you not much more valuable than they?" (NIV).

Father, don't let me forget the miracles You've done in my life. Help me to remember Your care and trust in Your provision. Thank You for the many times You've poured forth blessings.

Week Seven ~ God's Provision
Day 2: The Dollhouse

He provided for you so you would know that he is the Lord your God.
~ Deuteronomy 29:6 (NLT)

Sarah saved her money for months and accumulated quite a sum for a four-year-old. Concerned, it dawned on me I'd never talked with her about giving to God. I'd taught her the importance of saving for something she wanted—which happened to be a dollhouse—but hadn't taught her the importance of giving.

On the way to church I talked to Sarah about giving to God. I told her that she didn't have to give an offering of her little stash, but that it was important to begin developing a lifelong habit of giving back to God a part of what He blessed her with.

My sweet little girl agonized over her decision. She wanted to give money back to God, but had been saving faithfully, dreaming of buying the dollhouse I couldn't afford to purchase for her. I left the decision to her, but told her not to worry—you couldn't out give God. In the end she chose to dip into her savings and give God an offering. She seemed at peace with her decision, but I saw the struggle as she pulled the bills from her bank.

A few days later some renters who lived near us moved unexpectedly. When the owners of the house cleaned, they found children's toys left behind and piled them in a heap in front of the house for the garbage man to pick up. A friend came to visit and noticed the pile.

"Paula—there's a dollhouse!" she said. We grabbed Sarah's hand and ran up the block to the pile of discarded toys. In the middle sat a perfect dollhouse trimmed in pink siding, with a little button in the nursery that, when pushed, lit up the room and played a lullaby.

Sarah's eyes widened.

When we reached down to pick-up the dollhouse, Sarah pointed to several items next to it: a couple of dolls that fit the house, a fancy pink convertible, and dollhouse furniture. The three of us loaded the treasures into our arms and walked home. It didn't take long to sanitize the toys, and then Sarah and I rushed to the store where she spent her savings to finish furnishing the dollhouse.

God showed my little girl, firsthand, we can't out give God. Not only did He give more to my daughter than she could have purchased herself, but He gave her a priceless peek into His heart. He showed her He cared about her dream.

I had a similar experience as a child. I remember squirming in my seat at church as the usher collected an offering. I only had one dollar and didn't know when I would get another. I wanted to give something to God—but I had no change, nothing but that bill.

I fought with myself as the usher drew closer to my

seat. In my little girl heart I wanted to be bigger than my selfishness. I wanted to trust God with all I had. I struggled until the last minute, dropping the money in the plate just as it passed me.

Later that day, my grandma took me "out back" behind her house. I remember the creak of the screen door and the coolness of her covered back porch. "Now you don't need to tell anyone about this," she whispered as she slipped a dollar bill into my hand.

I remember looking down at the bill, wondering if she knew I'd given my last one at church, or if God had just whispered into her heart that He wanted me to have one. I never asked her—just took her gift, wrapped her in a hug, and thought about how you can't out give God.

Father, in this adult world of responsibility, when grocery bills, house payments, and mounds of needs demand constant attention, help me to remember Your heart toward me. Remind me that You haven't forgotten my desires. Touch me with Your personal attention and fill me with the grace to open my frightened hands as You lead, convinced that I can never out give You.

Week Seven ~ God's Provision
Day 3: The Dream

Remember the Lord your God. He is the one who gives you power to be successful.
  ~ Deuteronomy 8:18 (NLT)

Laundry piles loomed around me—not just three or four—maybe twelve or thirteen of them. Staring at the mess I asked God, again, to provide a washing machine. Mine had quit in the middle of washday, and we had no ability to replace it.

The telephone rang. I chatted a minute and hung up, dumbfounded. A friend purchased a new computer system and felt the Lord wanted me to have her old one. Was I interested? I laughed at the irony of it. I had prayed for a computer system until the washing machine broke, then abandoned that prayer to pray for the more pressing need.

Now, instead of a washing machine, God gave me a computer.

I'd just made a difficult decision to homeschool our firstborn, soon entering kindergarten. We'd always planned to homeschool our children, but I was pregnant (again), and after five years of nursing and diapers I realized how much it required to be home with little ones.

It consumed my life. My energy waned. My creativity got lost in the constant demands of menial tasks. My vocabulary was degenerating into something like, "Yes, nighty-night time. Give Mommy kiss!"

My dream to become an author lay buried under a sea of diapers and preschool books. To homeschool meant more years when the demands of mothering crowded out my personal hopes.

"What do you mean you're not sure?" My husband had asked when I pushed back. "We planned to homeschool before she was even born."

"Yes, but I don't think I can. With the baby coming and all I have to do . . . "

My husband said if we needed to rethink things we could, but once I was told it was okay to NOT homeschool, I couldn't back out. God had given us the desire to homeschool. To turn away from the choice would go against His will, the desires of my husband, and my own heart. I shelved my writing dreams once again.

That's when the computer system arrived.

It was as if God whispered to me as I sat in piles of dirty laundry, overwhelmed by the mundane tasks of the lifestyle I'd chosen, "I'm the keeper of your dreams, Paula. I know you want more than laundry piles. I gave you those dreams, and I'll see them through."

After God gave me the computer system I wrote poems about the children's discovery of the world, annual holiday letters, and page after page in my journal, but for five years I didn't pursue writing for publication. Instead, I went to the zoo, played patty-cake, taught little ones to read, and sought my Father's heart.

Then one day I sat down at the computer with no real plans. My fingers started moving and three months later I had a 500-page novel. Then I entered the world of writers — learning the craft of fiction writing, developing a website, launching weekly devotionals. The Lord began opening doors for publication and led me day by day to the next step on my writing journey.

When God gave me a computer system, I couldn't afford to buy, He not only answered a prayer, but also confirmed a dream.

God is like that. He doesn't only provide for my needs; He provides for my heart.

(Oh, by the way, we found a nifty washer/dryer set that even matched [hadn't had that for a while!] through the newspaper. He took care of my laundry, too.)

Father, thank You for providing for my heart. Even when I hesitate to ask You for what I need, much less what I want, You love and provide just the same. Give me the faith and courage to trust You with my needs and my dreams.

Week Seven ~ God's Provision
Day 4: The Blizzard

So I recommend having fun, because there is nothing better for people in this world than to eat, drink, and enjoy life. That way they will experience some happiness along with all the hard work God gives them under the sun.
~ Ecclesiastes 8:15 (NLT)

It'll be remembered as the blizzard of '96. For two days the airport was shut down. No one flew in or out. The vendors couldn't support the need for food for stranded travelers. Transportation even to the nearby hotels was impossible.

My husband and I were scheduled to fly out the first day the airport was operational after the blizzard. I'd prayed for months that the Lord would give me some special time alone with my husband before child number four arrived—the fourth child in six years. When my husband was invited to participate in a focus group at an insurance company's national convention, and I was invited to join him for an all-expense paid trip to a five star resort, we knew it was God's gift.

Waddling down the airport corridors, I ignored the

swelling crowds and repeated announcements of canceled flights. The baby, due in less than two weeks, didn't keep me from this trip. Certainly, God wouldn't let the weather ground me!

We reached our gate to discover our flight had been canceled. We were directed to the main terminal for flight reassignment. My courage waned. My husband kissed my cheek and whispered, "You've said this is from God. If it's His gift, don't you think we'll get to go?"

The happy ending to the story is that we miraculously made it on one of two flights that left for Phoenix that cold, winter day. We spent our mini-vacation in surroundings unlike anything either of us had experienced—a sunken tub in our $450 per night room, plush robes, fancy meals, and pristine pools where I simply raised a flag for my every need to be attended—all charged to the insurance company.

A few years ago God gave my husband and me another gift. We were in an incredibly difficult time financially. My husband had been laid off, and we were hanging on by a thread. During this struggle, I won a "gold" certificate to one of my favorite restaurants, and we enjoyed a night out, all expenses paid. There was no price limit on the certificate. I ordered desserts and lemonade and all the extras.

We felt rich.

My husband and I dreamed as we ate, talking again of our hopes for the future, something we'd been unable to do in the discouragement of unemployment. In that moment I heard the Lord whisper to my heart, "If you'll trust me, I'll give you these times of refreshment."

One of the hardest things about our choice to live on one salary has been my fear of not having the money for special times. As my husband chose employment based on protecting time for our family over salary level, fear escalated.

These two experiences show me God knows my need for refreshment, and His heart is much more generous than I ever understood.

Why, oh why, do I fight for myself—trying to give myself the things I think I lack? I have a Father who knows all I need and has the resources to take care of me—if I will only learn to rest in Him for the provision.

Teach me, Father, that You care about all my needs, even my need for pleasure and refreshment.

Week Seven ~ God's Provision
Day 5: Presence and Presents

The one thing I want from God, the thing I seek most of all, is the privilege of meditating in his Temple, living in his presence every day of my life, delighting in his incomparable perfections and glory.
> *~ Psalm 27:4 (TLB)*

It's a wonderful thing begin to grasp the concept of God as provider, but I suspect it's a life-long process. Jesus told us to think about how beautiful the lilies are and pointed out that not even King Solomon in all his glory was clothed as magnificently as they are. Still, despite the many gifts of provision I've experienced over the years I've not yet mastered the art of not worrying about money. I hope I'm better. Thankfully, the Lord continues to teach me.

This week I shared stories of incredibly wonderful gifts of provision. There were other seasons, too, when provision seemed far away. During the hard times the Lord often asked us, "Do you want Me or the gifts of My hand?" The obvious answer was I wanted both! But by looking deep inside I could honestly reply I wanted HIM more than anything else.

God continues to teach us He is trustworthy, both by giving miraculous provision and allowing hardship. Perhaps that is part of what the journey is about. He provided miraculously, showing us we could trust Him. Then, as faith grew, He asked us to trust Him in harder situations that lasted longer. One lesson He teaches as I mature in Him is sometimes He empowers me to surrender through sacrifice and obedience.

He's building spiritual muscle.

He's also deepening our love.

As I learn to trust Him I also learn to love Him. I realize that all the good this world has to offer doesn't compare to the wonder of knowing God intimately. As much as I enjoy His perks, they are nothing compared to experiencing relationship with Him. I don't want to be dependent upon His blessings. I want to be dependent on Him.

God's presents are amazing. But His presence is best.

Lord, I give You permission to refocus my life from Your blessings to Your Person. When the blessings come, I will praise You. In life's downs I will continue to seek You. Reveal more about who You are in the good times and bad. I want to know You more. The presents come and go, but You never leave me.

Awaken

Week Eight ~ Beautiful World

Week Eight ~ Beautiful World

Day 1: It Is Very Good

Then God looked over all he had made, and he saw that it was very good!
~ *Genesis 1:31 (NLT)*

The dirty gray of the winter streets paralleled my mood as I drove to pick up my daughter. It seemed every time I thought things would get better something else happened that wore me down. Disappointment after disappointment pounded like a relentless hailstorm. Now, sickness wound through our family, a never-ending cycle that left me exhausted and weak.

As I complained to the Lord about the hardships of this world I sensed something I couldn't quite grasp. It was as if He were whispering from Genesis. "And God saw all that He made, and it was very good" (NIV).

Hope flickered. But even as it began to burn it was almost snuffed out by a deluge of confusion. This world good? The idea went against the teaching I'd had about the fallen world. It went against my experiences in that season of struggle.

Yet, I knew it had to be a whisper from the Lord because I'd felt such peace and hope at the thought. And it was Scripture, after all.

I pondered this as my daughter climbed in the car. It was still on my mind when we stopped at the grocery store for a last-minute purchase for dinner. As we rushed through Safeway's wide doors in an effort to escape the cold, I suddenly halted. "Oh, look, sweetheart!" I breathed. The first display we came upon that dreary afternoon burst with sunshine. The table by the entrance was filled with vibrant yellow daffodils.

Jonquils, the smaller variety that grew near my childhood home, had always been a favorite. When I moved north, I planted daffodils along my front walk, reminiscent of the bright yellow patches of joy I watched for each spring as a young girl.

"Oh Lord," I whispered, "It IS very good."

God's goodness sings from each of His creations. I see His power in the majestic mountain peaks. His gentleness drips from a soft, pink rose. The ocean roars with His vast, unfathomable presence. His humor giggles out in a praying mantis. His loving strength wraps around me as I sit beneath the arms of a huge, leafy tree. Even a city of towering skyscrapers whose lights twinkle in a dark night shows God's love for us—how He delights in sharing with us a piece of His creative genius and lets us experience the joy of designing and building.

Too often, I focus on the muddy streets of life—both figuratively and literally. I see gray concrete instead of freshly fallen snow. I see litter on park grounds instead of lush green lawns.

I see disappointments instead of the victories.

Evil trampled on God's fair world, but it cannot wipe out its goodness. God wants us to enjoy the good world He created. I'm not just talking pessimism versus optimism. I'm talking about wiping away the grim of life to experience the good God intended for us to enjoy.

Won't you join me in the quest to embrace the goodness—the beauty—that our Father places all around us? Let's hunt for it, acknowledge it, rejoice in it! As we do we'll focus on the Creator and His goodness instead of the enemy's destruction. We'll discover more of God's personality. We'll experience more joy.

Wouldn't you know it? Those daffodils were on sale that day that started so dreary. It continued in a burst of sunshine—in my cart and on my daughter's face as we wheeled to the checkout counter!

Father, too often I see the ugly, the disappointment, the fallen. Show me how to peel away the film of filth the enemy has laid over Your creation. I want to focus on its goodness. Open my eyes to the beauty around me. Help me to find pieces of You in the good You've poured out on this earth.

Week Eight ~ Beautiful World

Day 2: Mountain Hike

As a deer gets thirsty
for streams of water,
I truly am thirsty
for you, my God.
   ~ Psalm 42:1 (CEV)

If I close my eyes and sit quietly, I can still feel it—the peace and beauty seeping into my soul. Watering it. Restoring me. Camping in the mountains has long been a favorite for me, and this experience was no exception.

I thrilled in cuddling my youngest boy as we sat next to the campfire watching the older boys whittle on sticks they'd found. Pride danced inside me as my oldest son chopped firewood and built fires. I enjoyed the creative expression of my daughter and her friends as they designed a whole new world out of stones, moss, and flowers.

We did all the typical camping stuff—roasted hot dogs, made s'mores, and took the children fishing. The best part for me, though, was the hike.

After three years of drought, the wet summer was a

welcome change, and our hike through the woods was a showcase for the effects of the moisture. Lush green lined the mountain path, layered with a rainbow profusion of flowers.

I wish I could describe the feast my eyes experienced—the lacy whites, bold yellows, and delicate pinks and purples cascading down the mountainside. I hadn't seen wildflowers like that for at least ten years.

Something deep inside felt nurtured. Even now I can close my eyes and reenter that wonderland. Occasionally, along the rugged trail, the trees would part exposing hazy mountain peaks in the distance. For a while a stream ran close to our path, dancing down the incline with gurgles and giggles.

When God's creation bursts out around me, singing in such lavish beauty, my heart involuntarily lifts to His. I've thought about this a fair amount since returning home to the city. I need to make times in nature a greater priority for my family and me. Walking in that mountain forest nurtured my spirit and blessed me with peace. It assured me of God's love and beauty.

God is always with me, but there are certain things that help me sense His presence. Nature is one of those. I also find Him in quiet moments of prayer, reading, and reflection, in times of singing and worshiping with fellow believers, and in good, deep conversations.

I have friends who feel close to Him when they dance before Him and others who talk to Him when they vacuum their carpet. My son says He feels God when he plays hockey. I can't relate to feeling God when I'm sweating and getting slammed against "the boards," but to each his own!

We each find Him in different places, feel close to

Him under different circumstances. I think the important thing is that we take the time to do those things that nurture our spirits.

Those amazing wildflowers were especially prolific during that camping trip because they drank up the rain that came in abundance. I'm reminded of another hike my husband and I took during the drought a couple of years before. The hot, dusty trail was lined with tired, brown grass. The little town we visited had posted "Pray for rain!" on church signs and bulletin boards. Those barren mountainsides couldn't drink. The water wasn't available.

It's different for us. The Living Water is always there. Sometimes we forget how thirsty we are and begin to shrivel under the cares of life. Other times, we know we're thirsty, but just can't seem to pull away from our busyness long enough to drink. The bloom of our life drops off the stem, leaving us barren. We must drink when we thirst or we can't blossom.

What nurtures Your heart? Where do you feel closest to God? Where can you go to get a good long drink?

Precious Living Water, make us thirsty for You. Reveal to our hearts where You want to meet us. Call us to Your side and flood us with Yourself.

Week Eight ~ Beautiful World

Day 3: The Party

In the time of those kings, the God of heaven will set up a kingdom that will never be destroyed.
~ *Daniel 2:44 (NIV)*

I could do nothing but stare.

Renoir's famous painting, "Luncheon of the Boating Party," exploded with beauty and color. Other visitors to the Art Museum pressed around me, listening to the tour guide explain its magnificence. They moved on but I didn't. I crept closer and sat on the floor. The joy of the masterpiece pulled me right into it. A security guard told me I needed to move, so I stepped back and waited until a bench behind me cleared. Then, I sat again, barely taking my eyes from the painting, and pulled out my journal and wrote:

> Lately, God has chosen to draw me closer to Himself by tiny glimpses of His vast and penetrating beauty. There is much of me that is pragmatic, practical, hardworking, and predictable. Today I sense the longing to find inner wells of beauty, emotion, and expression

I have not yet discovered.

There's something less tangible, more fleeting, and richer in transparent beauty that I long to uncover. I don't know what I mean by transparent beauty . . . an aura of Christ maybe? His scent, His love, the music that flows around His every move?

Yes, Christ is my Rock. He is solid and foundational. He is stable and trustworthy and dependable . . . But He is also wild . . . the essence of His beauty is tantalizing, fleeting; its breathy presence stirs a longing for more of Him and a longing for heaven.

Somehow, I want to touch His beautiful soul. I want to feel His gentle love, a whisper, a breath of fresh air stirring my own soul . . . a velvety touch on my skin, a wispy breeze across my face. There is beauty unexplored that I don't know how to find or express, but He has shown me tiny glimpses, and I thirst for more. (I suspect some of the deepest beauty can only be accessed by entering into His suffering . . . too often I allow pain to shut my senses down and harden my heart instead of allowing Him to use the emotion of the pain as a window, an open door to discover His beauty.)

Art critics make a big deal of the fact that "Luncheon of the Boating Party" combines three types of art: the still life, the portrait, and the landscape. They laud its composition, its brush strokes. I see something different. The lush fruit and sparkling beauty that bubbles in the crystal glasses of its still life, the joy of companionship in its portrait, and the mesmerizing beauty of its landscape hint of the joy of heaven.

That's why the Renoir affected me so. It pushed away life's discouragements and reminded me of what is to come. My yearning for the delights of eternity awakened, I pondered the beauty of God.

Someday we will party with Jesus. Food will spread in abundance. We'll laugh with our loved ones and drink in the beauty of creation untarnished. We will delight in all that is joyful, peaceful, and good.

Until then I want beauty to remind me of eternity and help me experience more of God's boundless beauty. God, in His gracious love, has placed much that is beautiful in this world. Some of it He created with His own hands, and other creations He allowed man to participate in. But each act of beauty points to Him. Each beautiful thing is a celebration of what is to come.

When I delight in Him, dream of sharing eternity with Him—when I feel my heart swell as I drink in beauty, isn't that worship?

Jesus, I know eternity with You will be beyond my most amazing dreams. I can't wait to experience beauty untarnished, perfect relationships that contain no pain, and all the joys You've planned for me. Each taste of something beautiful is a glimpse into Your magnificence. Whisper Your promise of eternity into my days, and help me find You in each thing of beauty I encounter.

Week Eight ~ Beautiful World
Day 4: The Sad Statue

I am the vine; you are the branches.
~ John 15:5 (NIV)

Renoir's fabulous painting, "Luncheon of the Boating Party" stood in front of me. Behind me sat a tiny bronze statue of Renoir's wife. The painting elicited a response of joy, but the little statue made me cry. I contrasted the vibrant woman in the painting with the grief I felt emanating from the sculpture.

Renoir painted "Luncheon of the Boating Party" when he was courting the woman who later became his wife. She sits front and center in the painting, her gentle, happy face full of tenderness and hope. Her nurturing heart shines forth in the way she interacts with a dog painted next to her.

The sculpture was made for her grave.

It depicts Renoir's wife as a young woman nursing their son. Instead of the awe of the hope of a new mother, I sense heaviness. To me, the little statue is worn and crushed, as if she knew the pain of her future. The young, hopeful woman in the painting became a weary, sad woman in the statue—a woman who saw the wretchedness of the world and the toll it would take upon her and her child.

It seemed to speak of all the pain that was to come—the tragedy of her husband's stroke and the grief of her sons' wounds in WW I. I mentioned my thoughts to the women next to me. They had just been discussing the same thing. "But isn't that what life does to you?" one of them said.

I wanted to reject the woman's words. They emanated hopelessness. Yet, they held an element of truth. I pulled out my journal and tried to process.

I hate what the world does to our dreams, vivacity, hopes, and tenderness. I don't want to become hardened and despairing as life takes its swipes at me.

I want to be a mother with hope, live to become a grandmother who still sings . . . a woman who hasn't lost the charm of a joyful, loving heart. I want to be a woman who brings beauty into this harsh world. Lord! Show me how to keep the flame of hope burning from my soul.

My mind went to a passage of scripture found in John 15:5. "I am the vine; you are the branches" (NIV). I scribbled in my journal:

This morning I read that Christ is the vine, and I am the branch. I can only hope to find color and beauty in this harsh world by staying connected to Christ and grasping, if only in brief moments, a whiff of His dancing heart, sweet smell, and effervescent beauty.

As I reflect upon this experience I ponder as a woman

who has known both the joy of fulfilled dreams and the crushing of unmet expectations.

There is much in life that makes me cry and tempts me to despair, yet the poor choices we humans have made have not squelched the beauty of a sunset, the innocent charm of a baby's smile, or the delicious fragrance of homemade bread.

I still gasp in wonder at the majesty of the mountains, the power of the ocean, or the sweetness of a bird's song.

As I embrace God's goodness reflected in the beauty He created, I realize I am not a pawn of my circumstances. I am not without hope. I am not a victim of cruelty, abandoned to this world of pain. God's care for me shines in the beauty all around me, waiting to be discovered.

And God's beauty shines in Christ.

I'm discovering Jesus. I'm finding Him more often than I used to. He's in a good movie, the night whispers, and the people I know. That discovery brings beauty that transcends the pain of the world.

In Him we have hope.

Father, I know life will continue to knock me around. I'll be angry and hurt, maybe even get mad at You when things don't go my way. But that doesn't change the fact that You are beautiful and good. May Your beauty change me, Lord. Open my eyes to it. Let it fill me with hope.

Week Eight ~ Beautiful World
Day 5: The Moon

It started when God said, "Light up the darkness!" and our lives filled up with light as we saw and understood God in the face of Christ, all bright and beautiful.
   ~ 2 Corinthians 4:6 (MSG)

My husband sighed and wrapped his arms around me as he shared the experience. "I came around a corner, and the moon was so breathtaking over the mountains I gasped. It was God catching me off guard with Himself."

"What do you mean?" I asked.

"Often I go through life as though it were routine. I experience good things and know they are from God, but I'm not awed. I miss the wonder of who He is.

"When I saw the moon, I literally had to catch my breath. It was so beautiful that all I could think about was how spectacular God is. It was as if He were showing me a piece of Himself—a little bit of His glory through creation. He shook me out of my routine and stunned me with His beauty."

Jerry's comments fit with something Brennan

Manning wrote in the *Ragamuffin Gospel* about how important it is for us to have a sense of wonder. He says that with the great scientific advances of the last century, and even the last ten years, we've forgotten how to be amazed. We just keep waiting for the latest invention or the most recent discovery, and we lose the wonder. He asserts that when we miss the amazement in life, we also miss a piece of God.

Another word for awe is reverence. Could it be that as we lose our fascination with His creation that we also lose some of our ability to reverence Him?

My husband's thoughts and Manning's writing encouraged me to ask God to open my eyes to the wonder around me. I'm glimpsing it in the laughter that bubbles forth unexpectedly from my little nephew as he bounces through my living room. I sense it in the roses blossoming in my front yard and the grace of my daughter as she does gymnastics. Acts of kindness can bring a lump to my throat as my heart swells at the wonder of good. Time spent exploring creation makes my heart lift in praise.

Years ago my family took a trip to California. As we returned home through Nevada, we saw the biggest, brightest, most amazing moon I've ever sense. The children were small, but even with their limited attention span they stared out the window, enraptured. I'll never forget how that gleaming white globe filled our windshield. We watched its slow ascent and marveled at its beauty.

Our sense of wonder led us to thoughts of God. My husband told the children the moon didn't have its own energy. It only reflected the light of the sun. He explained that the brightness we saw was the sun's light, bouncing off the moon, down to us.

We ended up talking about how we are like the moon. God shines His light on us and wants us to reflect it to the people we meet.

It was a holy moment, a moment of awe that became reverent.

I'm asking God to reveal more of His beauty to me. I first began praying like this because beautiful things have a way of touching my heart with a deep, peaceful joy. I wanted to see His beauty because it made me feel good, but I'm learning it does much more than that.

God's beauty is so pure, so awesome, so full of wonder that it brings us to our knees in reverence. As we worship Him, He changes us.

Father, I want to live life more fully with a sense of wonder. Open my eyes to the beauty You've placed around me. Give me a sense of awe as I see You in the good of people and the glory of creation. Then, Lord, please turn my awe to reverence that I might worship You with new depth and be changed.

Week Nine ~ I Am

Week Nine ~ I Am

Day 1: The God Who Is Present

God said to Moses, "I AM WHO I AM"; and He said, "You shall say this to the Israelites, 'I AM has sent me to you."
~ Exodus 3:14 (AMP)

Dedicated to Shay

"He is the God who calls Himself the I Am," she said.

I leaned forward. My children and I had been studying "I Am" verses thanks to an article I'd read. Now the concept was coming up at church. What more would God teach me about this name of His?

My friend said just when she thought her three-year battle with cancer was over, she'd been told it was likely the cancer had moved to her lymph nodes. She shared how she'd felt confused and angry. God met her by revealing Himself to her as the Great I Am.

Her comments sent me to the Bible that afternoon. I'd read the story in Exodus where God calls Himself, "I Am." I'd blazed past the text thinking God was simply communicating the fact of His existence, but as I read

Exodus 3:11–17 in several versions and browsed study notes and commentaries, my understanding expanded.

This is what I learned: When God says He is the I Am, He declares Himself as the God of the present who is always with us.

"God says His name is 'I AM' . . . Notice that it's present tense. God is always right now, in the present moment," writes Linda Joyce Heaner. "That means He has been 'I AM' in the past and will be 'I AM' in the future." *

God says it this way, "I am the eternal God" (Exodus 3:14, CEV).

The name God chose as His forever name is the one that declares His presence with us. The commentary in my NIV Study Bible says this name is, "the name that expressed his character as the dependable and faithful God who desires the full trust of His people."

Earlier in Exodus 3, God tells Moses, "I will be with you." According to study notes, the Hebrew verb translated "I will be" is the same as the one translated, "I am." It is used in Genesis 26:3 where God promises to be the sustainer and protector of His people.

Charles Ellicott writes, "God's name is His self-revelation."*

When God revealed Himself to Moses (and to the world through Moses' writing of Exodus), the one thing He wanted us to know is that HE IS.

No matter the heartache, the fear, the struggle, or disappointment, HE IS.

No matter the battle, HE IS.

And HE IS WITH US.

My friend finished her story this morning by telling us how God met her in her pain. She said as she cried she felt His arms around her. He held her tight and rocked her. And as He held her, He cried with her.

She said she's decided to quit asking "why" and to stop trying to figure out what she is supposed to learn from all the pain. She chooses to trust God loves her and is a good God, even when life doesn't feel good.

When we come to the end of ourselves—when life hits hard, like it has with my friend, God is there. Our I AM is the God of our present and the God of our future.

Because of Him there is hope.

Father, help me to remember You are the God who is with me in my now and who will be the I AM of my future. I'm never alone. Thank You that You Are the Great I AM.

*Creative Bible Study by Linda Joyce Heaner
**Ellicott's Bible Commentary: Volume 1*

Week Nine ~ I Am

Day 2: God Who Walked as Man

Jesus replied, "Philip, don't you even yet know who I am, even after all the time I have been with you? Anyone who has seen me has seen the Father! So why are you asking to see him?"
~ John 14:9 (NIV)

A friend raised in a strict Jewish home once told me she'd been taught never to use the words, "I am." Her family viewed those two words as too holy to repeat because God had used the two words to name Himself. He told Moses He was the great "I Am."

When Jesus said, "I Am," as He did several times during His ministry, He knew exactly what He was doing. With those words He declared Himself God (John 8). Later He explains that all He did on this earth showed the world who God really is.

I know people who feel Jesus can be trusted but who are afraid of God the Father. To them, Jesus is their Friend, a brother-type, but God the Father is a condemning, angry God, void of tender feeling, always judging them. He's scary or distant or plain 'ole mean.

When Jesus declared Himself as "I Am," He wanted us to understand that He and God were the same. The same patient understanding, the same compassion, the same sacrificial love of Jesus is who God the Father is as well.

In John 14:9, Jesus says, "Anyone who has seen me has seen the Father!" (NIV). He must have said it with some force, or maybe even exasperation, because in this translation the sentence ends with an exclamation mark, not a period.

This is important stuff.

As we come to know Jesus, we come to know God the Father. They are of the same heart! They are one!

Hebrews 1:3 says Jesus is the "exact representation" of God's nature. Colossians 1:15 says He is the "image of the invisible God" (NIV).

Many people mistrust God the Father because they had a bad experience with their earthly father. If he was abusive, they fear God. If he was hard to please, they feel they never measure up in God's eyes. If he was absent, they feel God is far away. If he was weak, they think God is weak. People who had good earthly fathers can go through this, too, mistaking the imperfections of their earthly dad as part of the Heavenly Father's character.

The enemy of our soul doesn't want us to truly know God. He surrounds us with experiences that confuse our understanding of who our Heavenly Father is. Even churches are sometimes so focused on telling us how to perform for God that their people are left with a picture of a Heavenly Father in the sky, making ugly tally marks next to our name when we mess up.

For the next several devotions we're going to look at descriptions Jesus used to help people understand who He is and what He came to do. As we come to know Christ's personality and purpose, it is important to remember that Jesus and God are alike. All those beautiful, compassionate things Jesus said and did represented God's personality and character to the world.

Father God, Help me know Your Son better than ever before. Give me a clear picture of who He is and why He came to Earth. And as He is revealed to me, please help me understand You better, too.

Day 3: The Way

Jesus answered, I am the way and the truth and the life. No one comes to the Father except through me.
    ~ John 14:6 (NIV)

I've dabbled in sign language. A specific movement comes to mind as I think about the verse where Jesus says He is the way. It's a sign that uses both hands, facing each other, starts at waist level, and moves forward. When I make this sign, I feel I'm symbolizing a road or a path.

Jesus is the road or path to God. He's the way to get from our human life—empty and alone—to a new spiritual life in relationship with our Creator. In fact, Jesus says He is the *only* way—that no one gets to God the Father unless they go through Him. This is also illustrated when Jesus says, "I am the door; if anyone enters through me, he will be saved" (John 10:9, NASB).

History shows us what Jesus did to provide the way to God. He died on a Roman cross and took the punishment for the sins of the world.

If we are to get close to God we must walk through

the door; go the one way that gets us to Him—through Jesus.

Jesus made the sacrifice. He provided the way. We simply receive the gift of an open door to God.

Romans 5 explains that we have peace with God because of what Jesus did for us. Peace means we have restored relationship, acceptance, and no more condemnation from the Father. It also says Jesus' act brought us into a place of highest privilege with God. In verse 10 it says we were restored to friendship with God.

It is important to remember that Jesus didn't talk God into this plan of offering Himself as a sacrifice. In fact, while facing the biggest trial of His humanity, He begged God to figure out a different way. But out of His love for the Father and His desire to see us restored to a loving relationship with the Trinity, Jesus surrendered to the pain and humility of a cruel death.

It hurt God to see His beloved Son killed on our behalf, but He loved us so much He prepared a way for us to be reconciled to Him: through Jesus. Romans 5:8 says, "But God showed His great love for us by sending Christ to die for us while we were still sinners" (NLT).

When Jesus said, "I am the way," He meant that He was the way to a relationship with the God of the universe and to gain all the privileges of those who are God's friends. If we choose to follow the way, Jesus Christ, we can "rejoice in our wonderful new relationship with God—all because of what our Lord Jesus Christ had done for us in making us friends of God" (Romans 5:11, NLT).

Jesus, I accept the gift of Your sacrifice anew in my heart. Thank You for being willing to be the way to God. I love You.

Week Nine ~ I Am

Day 4: The Truth

Jesus answered, I am the way and the truth and the life. No one comes to the Father except through me.
  ~ *John 14:6 (NIV)*

Have you ever been knocked flat? I have. Steamrolled by lies and crying under my covers I cowered like a wounded kitten, shaking and mewing in pain.

Guess what set me back on my feet?

Truth.

We live in an age where many people believe there is no truth. "What is truth?" They ask, then respond, "It's whatever you believe it to be."

If the Bible is quoted, they say, "That's *your* truth."

In many circles, the Bible is just a religious book, someone's *idea* of truth.

What do you believe?

Whether or not you accept the Bible as truth, I recommend you browse the history of the life of Christ. Read the book of Matthew or John and see how Jesus lived. Did He *live* truth?

Most folks believe His teachings are pretty smart—are true—even if they don't believe Jesus is God. Jesus showed a total lack of selfish interest. Power, prestige, control, money—none of that drove Him. He was motivated, purely and simply, by Love.

For most of us love is the Greatest Truth.

The traditional church embraces the Bible as God's truth. But even their perceptions can get in the way of understanding the fullness of truth.

Growing up in church I thought truth was synonymous with doctrine. Some churches had the full truth and others just had part of it. Truth was a list of doctrinal statements, usually focused on how my church was different than other churches.

I spent a lot of years working hard to live in the church's pet list of truth with a little "t," but those little "t" truths never did give me a relationship with the Father.

Jesus says HE is the truth.

That's quite a statement.

Do you believe it?

When Jesus first told the public why He came to Earth, He said He came to tell the good news to the poor, open blind eyes, relieve the oppressed, and set captives free. He came to offer big "T" truth—Himself!

God's enemy (and ours!) wove lies over the Father's creation. He told us all kinds of ugly things, like that God doesn't love us, that we have nothing to offer, that we're too full of faults to be loved or useful.

Jesus tells a different story in John 8:32. He says, "And you will know the truth, and the truth will set you free" (AMP).

Coupled with His declaration that HE is truth, this

Scripture takes on new meaning.

Truth isn't just a what; it's a who: Jesus Christ.

When we choose Jesus, we are set free from the oppression woven over our lives by the enemy of our soul. Jesus then offers relationship with us. In Christ we are never outcasts, forsaken, unloved, ignored, condemned, useless, or forgotten. We are included, embraced, loved, noticed, forgiven, useful, and remembered!

As we know Jesus and His love better, we understand who truth is, and the truth Jesus offers us is a freeing reality of unconditional love.

Chasing little "t" truths like formulas or pet doctrines can never set us free. Our performance can never break the spell of the lies the enemy has spent centuries weaving over our race. Only Jesus, the Truth, can dispel the lies and set us free.

Jesus, reveal Yourself to me as the Ultimate Truth and teach me to live in Your reality. By Your precious name, break the power of the lies that keep me from the fullness of Your truth.

Week Nine ~ I Am

Day 5: The Life

Jesus answered, "I am the way and the truth and the life. No one comes to the Father except through me."
~ John 14:6 (NIV)

Have you ever been told to "get a life"? If you're American, you've probably heard that statement, hopefully in the context of teasing. When someone tells you to "get a life," what he really means is: Find something important to think about/do. Quit wasting your time with stuff that is bogging you down or meaningless.

I find it interesting that Jesus says, "I am the life." What does He mean by that?

In John 14:6 Jesus is talking about how to get close to God the Father. I believe He is saying that HE is the way to eternal life. In John 11:35 Jesus says He's the resurrection and the life and that even if we die, we'll live forever because of Him. So, part of what He is saying is that He is the way to live forever with God. That's enough to knock your socks off!

But there's more.

In John 10:10 Jesus says, "I came that they might have and enjoy life, and have it in abundance (to the full, till it overflows)" (AMP).

I like how it reads in the *New Living Translation*. "My purpose is to give them a rich and satisfying life."

Lots of people live valuable, full lives—lives of love and service, but still miss the abundance of a relationship with their Creator. When you think about that word "life," is there anything more full, more abundant, than God?

Jesus wants to give us the most robust life possible, the life only He offers.

He wants to become our life. Our focus. Our every breath.

Relationship with Him becomes integral to who we are and everything we experience.

It is when we begin to discover Christ's depths, that we discover life, for He IS life.

I think I understood Jesus as the way when I was about seven. I heard that to live with God forever, you had to accept Jesus, so I did. I've known Him as the truth since my early 30's. While He has been the point of my life since childhood, I'm really only now discovering Him as the life. It began when I finally embraced Him as the truth, as I wrote about yesterday. That simple, but profound understanding took my life to a whole new level of living. I quit focusing on a little "t" to-do list and began focusing on Jesus.

I've only dipped my big toe into the ocean of life in Him—and this life is breathtaking. It is rich in love, dripping with beauty, and—sometimes scares the spit out of me. It's a crazy adventure that challenges and thrills me.

As we surrender to Jesus as our life, He ushers us into a grand adventure of relationship, self-discovery, and living from a place of love, faith, and passion.

When we begin to live in the wonder of who God is, we find overflowing, immeasurable life as we've never know it. The Bible calls Him the Bread of Life and promises if we come to Him we will no longer hunger or thirst. He'll fill us up. He is the very nourishment that sustains the life of our soul.

Jesus didn't only come as the entrance into relationship with God (the way). Nor did He only come as the One who sets us free by love (the truth), but He also came as the One who becomes our all (the life).

Jesus, help me to discover You as my very life.

Awaken

Week Ten ~ I Am II

Week Ten ~ I Am II

Day 1: The Bread of Life

Jesus replied, I am the Bread of Life. He who comes to Me will never be hungry, and he who believes in and cleaves to and trusts in and relies on Me will never thirst any more (at any time).
~ John 6:35 (AMP)

The scent of baking bread wafts through our home filling it not only with a pleasant aroma, but also with a sense of provision, warmth, and family.

During his single days, my husband would sometimes bake whole wheat bread as a treat for himself. After we married I learned to bake bread as a way to show him my love. I wasn't one of these women who could pull it off every day, or even every week, but whenever I did, it was certainly appreciated. As the children came, four of them in six years, baking bread was something I had less and less energy for. My sister-in-law decided we should own a bread machine, and she bought me one for Mother's Day. We were quickly hooked and have worn out several machines since that first one.

Even with the bread machine, I quickly tired of

keeping up with our family's demands for fresh bread. When my husband offered to become the primary bread maker, I relinquished the task willingly. A loaf doesn't last long in our home. When it's pulled, fresh and steaming, from the machine, we crowd into the kitchen. A whole meal can be made of bread, milk, and applesauce or bread, honey, and cheese.

Jesus calls Himself the Bread of Life. It's easy to make the application: Jesus is the very nourishment for our soul. Relying on His nourishment satisfies our spiritual appetite and need.

But I think there's more to this thought of Jesus as bread.

As I mentioned, I associate homemade bread with a sense of home—of provision, even love. Clustering around our kitchen table eating my husband's bread nourishes more than my body. It feels like family.

When Jesus says He is the Bread of Life, He invites us to feast on Him. He wants to be our family, our sense of home. He wants to be our life. We feast on Jesus by inviting His constant presence, by focusing on Him instead of trying to fill our hunger with other people or things.

Feasting on Jesus means we believe in Him, cleave to Him, talk to Him, think about Him, trust Him and rely on Him.

He isn't just a snack.

He is the nutrition that fills us.

He is provision for all our needs.

He is love to our hungry souls.

Unlike me, Jesus never runs out of the energy to provide the nourishment we need. In fact, He never grows weary (Isaiah 40), and He is so nourishing that we will never be hungry again (John 6).

That's quite a statement. When I eat of Jesus, I'll never have hunger again?

I've questioned that Scripture more than once. There have been plenty of times my heart has felt hungry, but what I'm discovering is the more I rely on Jesus—the more He becomes the very thing that sustains me, the less my heart rumbles and growls. The more at peace I feel. He satisfies my hunger to be completely and deeply loved, and no one can take that away from me.

Sometimes I feed my hunger with something besides Jesus. It might be as simple as grabbing a piece of chocolate when I'm sad or as complicated as turning to a relationship to fill the empty spot only Jesus can fill. When I turn to anything except Jesus, the result is whatever nourishment I've received (if I've received any!) quickly passes. Soon I'm hungry again.

The Jesus meals I ingest don't slip through my spirit. *They* aren't one time nourishment. They keep providing what I need days, weeks, and even years later.

Jesus says, "The one who makes a meal of me lives because of me" (John 6:57, MSG).

Let's make a meal of Jesus by relying on His provision for all our souls, spirits, and hearts need.

Father, in Your awesome, mystical way, fill my every hunger pang. Be my every meal. Help me to rest in Your presence and provision instead of turning to people or things that don't satisfy.

Week Ten ~ I Am II

Day 2: Light of the World

Later, in one of his talks, Jesus said to the people, "I am the Light of the world. So if you follow me, you won't be stumbling through the darkness, for living light will flood your path."
~ John 8:12 (TLB)

Our family likes to camp. I'm always stunned how quickly a tent grows pitch black, and how illuminating a flashlight is. When the flashlight is off, I can't see to find my socks, much less read a book or walk around without tripping over my children. But when the light is on, I can do any of that without even thinking about it.

When Jesus came to earth, He repeatedly called Himself the Light of the World. His actions shone brightly of love and grace. As the Light of the World, He also provided all the truth needed to find life in God. He says if we follow Him we won't stumble around, but we'll know where we're going.

In the big picture this is fairly easy for me to grasp. His truth shows me how to enter into relationship with God. It reveals how to live in grace and love.

It's in the little things, the daily living of a life of light where I struggle. I have bad habits and ways of relating to others that don't always shine of love or grace.

Sometimes I also feel I'm stumbling around, unsure of the path I should walk. I wish God would give me a big, swooping, all-encompassing answers to the hard decisions I have to make. I'd like God to turn on the bright light so I can see the whole picture and know my every move. Instead I often feel I have a tiny little flashlight that only illuminates only a small circle at my feet. I can barely see two steps ahead of me!

Why does He do that?

I'm sure He a lot of reasons. I have figured out one thing, though. If He gave me all-encompassing answers to certain questions, I wouldn't spend as much time with Him. I'd grab my marching orders and run off to do them instead of seeking His wisdom, step-by-step. When there are no clear-cut answers, I seek Him more. When I do that, we hang out together more. I get to know Him better, discovering how He thinks and moves.

There are times He turns on the floodlights. That holds its own challenges for me. It's like He illuminates a huge, open space, inviting me to run free. Sometimes that feels overwhelming, and I wish for the little circle at my feet. But He's in the open spaces, too, cheering me on, encouraging me to explore in freedom.

I'm glad Jesus came to Earth and illuminated the whole world with a brand-new way to think about God and life. I'm thankful for the times He lights our steps, one little circle at a time. I'm excited about the times He turns on the floodlights and encourages us to run free.

Jesus, help me to enjoy walking with You as You illuminate each little step. When You shine light on a bigger space, help me to have the courage to run free in it. Thank You for knowing what amount of light is needed in each situation. I'm grateful there's not a single moment I'm without Light.

Week Ten ~ I Am II

Day 3: The Gate

*I am the Gate for the sheep. All those others are up to no good—
sheep stealers, every one of them. But the sheep didn't listen to
them. I am the Gate. Anyone who goes through me will be cared
for—will freely go in and out, and find pasture.*
~ *John 10: 7–9 (MSG)*

Our family's old blue tent is a huge cavern of canvas that
sleeps all six of us. When the children were younger, my
husband, Jerry, always positioned himself by the tent door
when we camped. Anyone who tried to get to his family had
to come through him first. We felt safe knowing papa bear
stood guard between the world and us.

In our tent we had our own little community.
Everyone there belonged to each other. We were family. If
someone needed to go outside during the night, he (or she)
went with Jerry, who carried a flashlight and showed him
safely to his or her destination. He saw our needs were met.

Sometimes we camped with family or friends. Once
that tent flap was zipped, entrance was only for those whose
voice Jerry recognized. He'd readily allow a young cousin or

friend to join our little tent community, but he didn't welcome strangers.

Jesus calls Himself the Gate or the Door. In this passage He's using the image of a shepherd to explain Himself. In Eastern culture the sheep were often kept in natural pens made of rocks or caves. A shepherd who took care of his sheep would literally sleep lying in the opening to the pen. Anything that came into the fold had to go through the shepherd.

The shepherd chose who was welcomed into his community and protected his sheep from those who would harm them. His sheep knew and trusted him. He freely led them in and out of the pen, finding water and good pasture. He took care of them.

When Jesus claims to be the Gate, He is explaining He is the way to join God's family. He is also promising to protect those in His care and to show them how to live life as a part of His community.

I like the image of Jesus that comes to mind as I remember my husband sleeping by the flap of our tent. Jesus is always there, protecting us and offering Himself as the leader of our family. He sleeps in the tent with us, giving us a chance to get to know His ways and learn the sound of His voice. He knows His way around the campgrounds of life. He walks with us, carrying the flashlight to illuminate the paths He chooses.

Jesus, thank You for offering Your very self as a living, breathing entrance into to Your family. Thank You that You also give Yourself in relationship. You protect me, help me know You, and show me the best way to go.

Day 4: The Gate II

I am the Gate for the sheep. All those others are up to no good—
sheep stealers, every one of them. But the sheep didn't listen to
them. I am the Gate. Anyone who goes through me will be cared
for—will freely go in and out, and find pasture.
    ~ John 10: 7–9 (MSG)

Sometime during what was supposed to be a safe, fun
evening, my son's new $100 hockey stick disappeared. We
enjoyed the company of parents and kids at a picnic for
those involved in my son's hockey club. It was a wonderful
evening of friendship, and we participated in all kinds of fun
activities, from baseball, to hockey, to lots of food. It was
especially upsetting when the stick disappeared because we
trusted this community. What made it worse was my son
won the stick at a tournament as a reward for being chosen
tournament MVP, so it held extra value for him.

When Jesus talked about being the gate for the sheep,
He included His concerns about thieves who would come
and harass His sheep, stealing from them the good life He
had planned.

He says, "I tell you the truth, the man who does not enter the sheep pen by the gate, but climbs in by some other way, is a thief and robber" (John 10:1, NIV). Later he says, "The thief comes only to steal and kill and destroy; I have come that they may have life, and have it to the full" (John 10:10, NIV). Jesus knew the danger of someone sneaking into His special community with the intent of stealing and destroying it.

How do we identify a thief in the sheep pen? We watch how he enters, and we study the results of his efforts. Does he come to us in the grace of Jesus? Do his words/actions dominate us or lead us with love? Does he encourage unity, bringing healing and kindness, or do we grow thin and spiritually ill under his counsel?

Sometimes thieves come as thoughts. We recognize these enemies the same way—by their fruits. Thoughts that take away peaceful, joyful, abundant living are the bad guys, trying to slip into the fold. Major thought thieves include inadequacy, shame, condemnation, guilt, rebellion, lust, doubt, and unforgiveness. Those kind of thoughts come out of experiences or teaching when our hearts were not being shepherded by the grace of Jesus. They rob us of our peace and try to keep us from living in sweet communion with Jesus.

Sometimes we unknowingly allow our hearts to be shepherded by seemingly good things that are actually robbers. We do this when we rely on anything or anyone but Jesus. Financial security can be a blessing, but when attaining it becomes our focus, we are allowing ourselves to be shepherded by something that doesn't satisfy. Our jobs, ministry, and service to our families can be a beautiful outgrowth of time with our Shepherd, or they can become a controlling taskmaster, robbing us of our relationship with Jesus by stealing our time, energy, and self-confidence.

Next time you feel your joy ebbing away, ask yourself if there just might be a thief in the sheep pen.

Jesus, too often I don't recognize thieves when they come to steal from me. Help me to be more perceptive and to call out to You when something or someone tries to rob me of the abundant life You want me to lead. Give me clarity and wisdom so I know how to deal with each situation, and help me to get out of the way so You can chase them off with Your Shepherd staff.

(BTW, we found that hockey stick—guess someone put it away in the wrong place.)

*Note: Most commentators connect Jesus' teaching in John 10 with God's words in Ezekiel 34:2–31 where He expresses anger at the false shepherds that didn't care for His sheep. He said when the robbers were in charge His people grew thin and sick and were dominated, left in bondage, scattered, and out of community. God promises in Ezekiel 34 to be a Good Shepherd, to heal His sheep and to "deliver them from all the places in which they were scattered on a cloudy and gloomy day." You might enjoy reading about God's promises to care for his sheep in Ezekiel 34.

Week Ten ~ I Am II

Day 5: The Good Shepherd

I know my own sheep, and they know me.
~ John 10:14 (NLT)

I have a good friend whom I know mostly by email. We've only seen each other a couple of times, but our understanding of each other and our care for one another has blossomed over the Internet.

She told me that in recent years she'd become a bit of a hermit, hiding her heart and protecting herself from relationships, but about a year ago God began to give her good friends online. This contact wasn't as scary for her as face-to-face contact would have been.

Now that she's opening to friendship, He is gently prodding her to come further out of hiding and develop relationships with people in her local community.

Her testimony reminded me that Jesus is a wonderful, tender shepherd of our hearts. The Lord didn't push my friend immediately into community. He led her, one step at a time, teaching her to trust His voice and asking her to take increasing risk as her ability to follow Him grew. Like a tender, wise shepherd He didn't move her too fast for the emotional wounds she'd experienced. Instead, He healed her as she could receive His truth and guided her forward as her heart was able.

It's the picture of the Good Shepherd with a little lamb. The lamb, wounded, couldn't walk by itself. The Shepherd bound the lamb's wound and carried her where she needed to go, whispering into her ear how precious she was to Him. The little lamb learned the tenderness of His voice and how to distinguish it from the pushy, hurtful voices she'd listened to before getting to know the Shepherd.

The little lamb was also timid around the other sheep. One sheep had hurt her deeply, and she believed the lie that she was unworthy to befriend the flock. The Shepherd kept the lamb close as she learned to walk on wobbly legs and talked to her not only of how much He loved all His sheep but also of how the little lamb had something beautiful to offer the others.

The lamb grew more confident and began to talk with the other sheep and to discover the beauty of friendship as well as the gifts within herself that she could offer to others.

My friend is that little lamb in the Shepherd's arms. So are you and I. The beautiful thing about the Good Shepherd is He knows exactly what each of us needs. He knows the perfect timing for each new step He wants us to take as well as when we need to rest awhile in green pastures beside still waters (Psalm 23).

Jesus says in John 10:14 that He knows His sheep, and we know Him. There are times that instead of listening to the voice of the Good Shepherd, who knows and cares for our hearts, we listen to the thieves and robbers who sneak into the sheep pen. (See yesterday's devotional).

Sometimes we forget the true character of our Shepherd and push away His gentle staff of prompting, believing Him to be uncaring, untrustworthy or unloving. But as we recognize our fear and rebellion and cry out to Him, we discover He is waiting patiently for us to be ready to move forward. He knows sometimes we're afraid and our hearts are fragile, so He leads us a step at a time, as we are strong enough to follow.

Over time we learn the Shepherd's voice and walk close to Him in more and more confidence. He shows us how to trust Him and let Him lead us into the best plans for our life.

My precious Good Shepherd, please give me a more complete understanding of what You want to do in my life. Make me wise with spiritual wisdom so I can live in ways that honor You. Help me do good, kind things for others. As I grow like this, I want to get to know You better and better. Please strengthen me with Your glorious power so I will have the patience and endurance I need. Help me to be filled with joy, always thanking You for bringing me into Your fold and promising me an inheritance with Your holy people who live in the Light. Thank You for rescuing me from the one who rules in darkness and seeks to wound me. Thank You for purchasing my freedom with Your blood and forgiving my sins. (This prayer a paraphrased version of Colossians 1:9–11.)

Awaken

Week Eleven ~ Deeper

Day 1: Grasping the Vine

I am the vine, you are the branches. He who abides in Me, and I in him, bears much fruit; for without Me you can do nothing.
~ *John 15:5 (NKJV)*

I longed to understand what Jesus meant when He said I should abide in Him. I memorized John 15:5 and hung the Scripture on my wall where I could see it daily and meditate upon it. But I still didn't get it. Digging deeper I studied multiple versions of John 15:5. The *New International Version* told me to "remain" in Christ. *The Living Bible* said, "Take care that you live in me, and let me live in you."

When I asked God to show me how to abide in Him, I embarked on a journey with no end. I continue to discover new depth to abiding in Christ as I learn to *live* in Him.

Early in my quest to understand abiding a speaker helped me gain insight. He said abiding in Christ meant to be "centered" or "grounded" in Jesus. Christ is our foundation.

I pondered how to let Christ be my foundation. It meant everything in my life pointed back to Him. I needed to build my life around my relationship with Him, living with Him each day, never compartmentalizing Him. He wasn't just God for church or Someone to take off the shelf when I needed help. He wasn't only a bedtime prayer or grace before meals.

Abiding meant trusting Him and inviting Him into all of my life.

It meant my life revolved around Him.

Intellectually, I grasped the idea that to abide in Jesus meant to keep my focus on Him, to spend time with Him, and to let Him be my foundation. I understood my efforts were worth nothing if I wasn't being nourished and directed by Jesus. But intellectual understanding stops short of real living. And God, being God, allowed me to experience things in life beyond my control so I could begin to live the concept.

The Father is gentle with us. Abiding 101 came in the form of a new job. It was a good place to get my feet wet. As Director of Children's Ministries for a growing church, I constantly dealt with situations I couldn't fix by sheer hard work, one of the biggest being staffing the children's department. I couldn't get enough volunteers by talking to people, doing presentations, or team building. I learned to lean completely on the Lord to supply our needs. I believed that He loved those kids more than I did and decided my main recruiting strategy would be prayer. Determined not to wring my hands over the empty spots on the team, I leaned harder into Jesus when the gaping holes cried out for filling.

In less than two years our little church more than doubled, and God staffed two services of full children's programming. I survived the stress of that part-time job because God taught me to abide in Him, to spend time with

Him, to lean on Him for my needs.

Abiding 101 began a journey through the School of Deepened Understanding which intensifies with each new class. I'm still traveling through this particular university, and I understand I won't get my diploma until I cross from this world to the next.

That's okay.

I want to continue this course of study because it is where I get to know my Best Friend.

I invite you to peek over my shoulder for the next few devotionals as I explore what I've learned and what I want to learn. But don't just watch. Join in! It can be scary because living more fully in Christ often means living less in a world we control.

But I promise it's worth it.

If you're already enrolled in the Academy of Abiding, tell the Lord you're willing to go deeper. If you've never asked Him to teach you how to abide in Him, take the plunge and enroll today!

Deeper, deeper in the love of Jesus daily let me go! Higher, higher in the school of wisdom, more of grace to know. Oh deeper yet I pray and higher every day and wiser blessed Lord in thy precious Holy Word. (Prayer taken from an old hymn, "Deeper, Deeper," by C. P. Jones)

Week Eleven ~ Deeper

Day 2: Remain

Deeper, deeper, tho it cost hard trials,
deeper let me go! Rooted in the holy love of Jesus,
Let me fruitful grow.
  ~ "Deeper, Deeper," by C.P. Jones, Verse 3

I have loved you even as the Father has loved me. Remain in my
love.
  ~ John 15:9 (NLT)

The pain seared, a burning fire making my heart race with irregular beat, my stomach churned, crying out for relief. If only it were a virus so I could throw up and ease the pain! But emotional suffering isn't so easily dealt with.

Thoughts zoomed through my mind. The Scriptures that could hold them in check seemed to race after them with red lights blaring, like tiny police cars unable to catch up to the thieves stealing my peace.

I shoved back the covers and headed for my recliner. Usually time in prayer with journal and pen in hand helped me process. Only the words wouldn't come this time. I slipped back to my husband's bedside hoping he'd wake up and hold me again, pray for me. But he didn't, and I couldn't bring myself to interrupt his rest.

I flopped back in the recliner. "Lord! I need you. Help!"

But I didn't hear His voice.

No answer came.

Or did it?

An overwhelming desire to go outside filled me. I wanted to lie in the hammock and look at the stars. I questioned myself. It was after midnight and cold that time of year. The pull persisted. Wrapped in my fluffy robe I grabbed a pillow and the blanket off the recliner and padded into the night air.

Cocooned in the hammock, swaying gently, I became part of something bigger than myself. The wind rose and whooshed through the tree and the stars twinkled in the sky. It took a while, but eventually my heart rate returned to normal, and the pain in my stomach eased. The thoughts quit whirling and let me be. Still, no words came, no amazing prayers, no working through the issue.

Only quiet.

And then they began, soft melodies of worship, slipping from my mouth, responding to the Creator of stars and night wind. I sang to Him as the tree, dark shadows of leaves and limb above me, danced in the breeze.

I didn't understand that night that I'd just experienced another class at the University of Abiding. I knew only that though I couldn't process the pain of the situation or answer the questions of what I'd done wrong or right, I was comforted by focusing on Him. In my worship I surrendered to His deity and remained in the truth that He cared.

When John 15 talks about abiding in Christ, it includes a verse which says God loves me the same as He loves Christ. Then it says to remain in His love. I'd never made the connection until that experience.

Part of abiding is remaining in Love.

He loves me. When others accuse or attack. When I fail. When I succeed. When I question the things I do or the person I am.

He loves me.

Learning to abide in Christ means nothing convinces me otherwise.

God is still God when life stinks.

His Love is as near as our very breath and big enough for all we face.

Father, help me remain in Your love as life knocks me around like a massive ocean wave, tossing and tumbling me about. Help me rest in the embrace Your love when I am too tired to fight the onslaught of pain. Help me to drink of You, eat of You, Jesus, sating my thirst and receiving nourishment from this one truth: You love me.

Week Eleven ~ Deeper

Day 3: Fruitless Effort

No branch can bear fruit by itself; it must remain in the vine.
   ~ John 15:4 (NIV)

Have you ever heard a grape grunt and groan as it grew?
   Of course not.
   A few years ago I heard a speaker who pointed out that we do this all the time. We strive, grunting and groaning, trying to produce spiritual fruit.
   But fruit can't make itself grow. It only grows because it is connected to the nourishment of the vine.
   The truth of the speaker's words blared like a bullhorn as I listened to this new thought.
   In the past I would have beat myself up for not working harder to stay attached to The Vine. I would have assumed my grunting and groaning meant I wasn't trying hard enough to be close to Jesus. I should pray and read my Bible more. There was even a time I thought bearing fruit meant a tally list of how many people had come to Jesus because of me, how many church committees I'd served on, and how many jobs I'd done well for God. Somehow I had

missed the verses saying the fruit of the Spirit is love, joy, peace, patience, kindness, goodness, faithfulness, gentleness, and self-control.

That was all BEFORE.

Before I understood grace.

Before I grasped God's commitment to me.

I don't have to work to stay hooked up to The Vine. My Lord, The Vine, is holding onto me.

Sure, I still try to hold onto God, but He's so big I can't! He is the One who does the holding, placing gentle arms about me.

Jesus says His yoke is easy and His burden is light, (Matthew 11:30, NIV), or as it is stated in *The Message*, Jesus says, "Keep company with me, and you'll learn to live freely and lightly."

When I become a grunting, groaning piece of fruit, it is often because I've taken upon myself the job of the Holy Spirit. I'm working really hard to bear fruit. Focused on my failures I try to remake myself. The problem is the more I focus on my faults the more I seem to live them! Life becomes a burden and I feel beaten down by the yoke of right living.

That isn't the Lord's plan. He wants me to walk in the freedom of His grace. I did nothing to earn my salvation, and I can do nothing to sustain it. He is the one that takes this faulty vessel and refashions it in His image.

And how does He do that? By teaching me to lean hard on Him.

As I abide in Him, I get to know Him.

As I focus on who He is, I become like Him.

Our long season of great financial difficulty brought this concept closer to home. I wanted to trust God to provide for our family, but found it much easier to take my credit card to the grocery store than to sit home and pray for food. I lived in a continuous cycle of failure, guilt, and confession. I strove for more self-control in my spending, but the more I focused on my inability to trust God's provision, the more desperate I was to buy the things we needed. I finally told the Lord, "I just can't do this. All I know to do is to fling myself upon your mercy, not because I deserve it, but because mercy is part of your character."

As I felt the full impact of a behavior I couldn't control, I discovered the truth that the Lord's mercies are new every morning (Lamentations 3:21–23). I learned to abide in grace instead of walking in guilty failures, accepting His mercy in my inadequacies.

Gradually, peace replaced desperation, and God revealed His heart for me as He refined the fruits of mercy and forgiveness in my life.

I'm glad we don't have to be grunting, groaning, striving fruit. We simply hang on the vine drinking in God's nourishment, which gives us what we need to change. God showers us with love, puts His own nature within us, and walks with us through the daily struggles of life.

Father, I don't ever want to work at bearing fruit again. I want to rest in You and let You produce the goodness in me that You promise. Please give me the beautiful, luscious fruits I see in You. Nourish this fruit that clings to the Vine.

Week Eleven ~ Deeper

Day 4: Ouch!

Every branch that bears fruit, He prunes it so that it may bear more fruit.
> *~ John 15:2 (NASB)*

Deeper, deeper! Blessed Holy Spirit,
Take me deeper still,
Till my life is wholly lost in Jesus,
and His perfect will.
> *~ "Deeper, Deeper," by C.P. Jones, Verse 2*

Have you ever been pruned?

I have. Did you like it?

Me, neither!

At least at first.

I'm been through relational pruning, financial pruning, church pruning, and work pruning. In many of those situations I elevated something or someone over Him. I looked to these things or people for happiness, security, and self-esteem. It's not that I meant to. In fact, I didn't even know I had until it was pruned away.

There were relationships where I tried so hard to please the person I missed God's will for my life, elevating people's plans for me over His. I thought finances could make me feel secure, but when they were gone I found security came only from Jesus. Without realizing it I allowed church ties to dictate doctrine, and I missed some of the most beautiful truths in Scripture.

Of course, I'm not saying that every loss is pruning. But, looking back on my life, many losses were. The process of pruning only cuts away what is unnecessary or what impedes healthy growth. Pruning never means being cut from the Vine.

I don't like being pruned. Yet even as He cuts people and things away He holds tightly to me. I don't walk through the experience alone because His love always remains. After the pruning the Good Gardener wraps my wound and binds me to the Vine. After a while the loss hurts a little less because the nourishment from the Vine is flowing more strongly through me.

The cutting helps me focus more passionately on my Savior. I feel more distinctly my desperate need for His nourishment, and I drink in big gulps instead of little sips.

Sometimes it feels like pruning means the Lord is mad or doesn't like what we are. It's really the opposite. He prunes because He likes the fruit He sees and wants more! He prunes so we can become peaceful, secure, strong people, rooted in Him. He prunes to set us free to taste the sweet depth of His love.

After pruning we become more fruitful. Our lives are more focused on the Lord. Joy buds. Peace grows and blossoms. Perseverance blooms. And then we awaken to a sense of the solid foundation of abiding that undergirds our life.

It feels like the arms of Jesus.

Lord, sometimes I fight Your pruning. I see the hurt and not the plan You have for good. I complain, whine, and cry. Sometimes I even doubt Your love for me. I tell myself You don't care. But all the while You bind my wounds and pour nourishing love into what remains of me. Thank You that I never go through this process without Your love. Give me the ability to submit to Your pruning shears and trust You know best. I give You permission to prune away. Just hold me REAL tight. Okay?

Day 5: Tender Places

Deeper, deeper every day in Jesus,
Till all conflict past,
Finds me conqu'ror and in His own image
perfected at last.
> ~ *"Deeper, Deeper," by C.P. Jones, Verse 4*

There's an on-going situation in my life that is very painful. I pray often that the Lord will fix it or show me a better way to handle it. So far, it hasn't changed. I just hold onto my Father's hand and walk through it.

Sometimes this situation strikes hard and fast. It jumps out at me from behind the door where it always lurks. It assaults my heart with flawless precision and attacks my mind with fears. Other times it is a quiet, ever-present ache. The pain lives in my heart, hauntingly sad. I walk with it. Fighting only causes more hurt. I accept the empty hole and turn my gaze toward more pleasant vistas.*

Perhaps this is the most important lesson I've learned so far in the University of Abiding. There are things in this life that hurt. Sometimes they hurt for a long time. They attack the most tender places and mock trust in God. But no matter how much they taunt they cannot change one fact.

I hang from the Vine. Never alone, I am always hooked up to Jesus' nourishing love. My God waters me, feeds me, prunes me, and enjoys me. God chooses to be in this earthy garden with me when all common sense says He should just hang out in heaven's garden where it is perfect and safe.

But He wants to walk through life with me. He wants to stay connected.

We can't always find hope in the circumstances we face. But Hope is there when we abide. He never goes away. He never disconnects. He never decides the road is too long or that we were just bad apples anyway.

Father, thank You that I can rest in You, abiding in Your love, no matter how difficult life becomes. Thank You that I am not without hope because I am never without You. Let my life be to Your glory as You produce within me the many fruits that grow out of abiding.

*Friend, this devotional was written years ago. I still believe in its truths enough to keep it here for your journey. But I also want to offer the perspective of the passage of time. This situation hasn't changed significantly, but my Sweet Jesus has tended the wound over the years and ever-so-gently asked permission to remove the sadness. Some pain is deep. Connected to self-concept and trauma, this pain must be wisely healed, in perfect timing, or the process of healing can actually cause more damage. Be patient with yourself in your deep wounds. Offer them to Him to heal in His way and time. I talk more about this in Volume 4 of the *Soul*

Scents devotionals. That volume is called *Flourish* and much of its content was written more than ten years after I penned many of the devotions found here in *Awaken*.

Week Twelve ~ Celebrating Grace

Day 1: A Whole New Way of Living

Sin and despair, like the sea waves cold,
Threaten the soul with infinite loss;
Grace that is greater, yes, grace untold
points to the refuge the mighty cross.

Grace, grace, God's grace,
Grace that will pardon and cleanse within,
Grace, grace, God's grace,
Grace that is greater than all our sin!
> ~ *"Grace Greater Than Our Sin," Text by*
> *Julia H. Johnston, Verse 2 and Refrain*

With Christ's obedience to the cross came a whole new perspective to our relationship with God. As the calendar counts toward the celebration of Christ's death and resurrection, my heart is awed by the changes this act of ultimate sacrifice ushered in.

The stories of the Old Testament show a lot of law-centered activity. Instead of being empowered by an indwelling God, Old Testament believers struggled with hearts the Bible calls deceitful and desperately wicked (Jeremiah 17:9).

Though a merciful God provided a system of annual sacrifices so the people could push their sins forward year after year, religion was increasing built upon rituals and rules, far more than God Himself initially commanded. Man interpreted God's instructions adding law upon law to the original intent.

After the incarnation and resurrection everything changed.

Jesus taught of a new way. He told his disciples his yoke was easy and His burden was light. When Christ died He took our every sin upon Himself and canceled it.

Gone.

Forever.

Then, wonder of wonders, the God who became human and walked among us, moved inside and cleaned us up, sending an advocate to live *within* us (John 14).

God gave His followers a new heart, replacing the heart of stone, the one that had been desperately wicked, with a heart that desires the things of God (Ezekiel 11:19; Jeremiah 31:33; Hebrews 10:16).

Instead of a religion of striving to be good but never living up to a mountain of expectations, God offers a new way, the way of the indwelling Spirit. This new way is based upon words like forgiveness, love, trust, guidance, and empowerment.

Now, His followers are never condemned (Romans 8:1). They are offered love and mercy, set free from the law of sin and death (Romans 8:2), and invited to enter into His rest (Hebrews 4). As we keep our eyes on Jesus, the author and perfecter of our faith, the Holy Spirit transforms us into the image of Christ (Hebrews 12:2; 2 Corinthians 3:18).

Unfortunately, religion today often does what it did with the Israelites of old. Man interprets God's wisdom adding more rules and boxes than God intended.

It's such a comfort to realize we can trust God to make us what He wants us to become. We can let go of religious culture and lean instead into our Savior's loving arms. In God's own way and time He will complete the good work He started in us (Philippians 1:6).

Christ's birth, death, and resurrection ushered in a whole new way of living.

Thank you, Jesus, for humbling Yourself and coming as little child. For walking the Earth and showing us the new way. For surrendering to death so that we might live in intimacy with You forever. Thank You for coming as Spirit in our very selves and empowering us to walk out the new lifestyle You offer. Teach me to rest in Your miraculous work of cleansing and empowering. Help me trust You to make me all You want me to be.

Week Twelve ~ Celebrating Grace

Day 2: Disney Got It Right

Out of his fullness we have all received grace in place of grace already given.
   ~ John 1:16 (NIV)

Disney's movie *Enchanted* got it right. It isn't healthy to ignore genuine emotion.

In the fairy tale an animated princess falls through a well and pops into real-life America. No longer a cartoon, a flesh-and-blood woman, Giselle (played by Amy Adams), mets a flesh-and-blood man, Robert (played by Patrick Dempsey).

Robert is appalled to learn that Giselle is marrying a man she just met. Giselle believes the man is Prince Charming, that they fell in love while he sang to her, and this is all that is necessary to start a life with him. Incredulous, Robert talks to Giselle about real relationship, which includes knowing each other's likes and dislikes, dreams and struggles. He says real love includes conflict and real emotion, and she isn't facing reality with all her happy singing and surface emotion.

Later in the story Giselle gets mad at Robert. She expresses her anger; then in a moment of insight she says, "I'm mad!"

We laugh as she dances through the room repeating, "I'm mad! I'm mad!" and giggling.

I resonate with this scene because I've struggled with feeling okay with being mad. My go-to response was to feel guilty and blame myself for problems rather than admit genuine anger. As I began to understand anger is an appropriate response when one is hurt, I had a real life Giselle moment. I drew a boundary that was not well-received. The other person heaped on the guilt and demeaned me. As I walked away, I felt angry at how I'd been mistreated. The old me would have blamed myself for not being kind enough or good enough. I'd be consumed with guilt for letting the other person down.

The new me was angry.

My brother and I were together when this incident occurred. When we were clear of the other person, I practically danced with joy. Like Giselle my declaration of "I'm mad!" was a declaration of freedom. I told my brother. "I can't believe it. I'm *mad!* It's the appropriate emotion when mistreated!"

The painful exchange became a celebration of grace.

Living in a grace-filled culture gives room for appropriate emotion. Living with God as one covered by grace gives room for normal emotion as well.

One time I struggled with the Lord, trying to work through a deep issue. As I journaled I felt Him prompt, "You're angry with Me, Paula. Why don't you just admit you're mad instead of feeling guilty about the emotion you're trying to hide. It'll save us a lot of time."

In relationships of grace we are free to have normal emotions, even with God. He is not afraid of our anger. In fact, he'd rather us be real and blurt out what we feel than try to "nice" it up like a "good little Christian."

Our position as beloved of God is based on what Christ did at the cross. His behavior, not yours or mine, establishes safety. Once covered in the blood of the Precious Lamb, Jesus, we are never condemned or rejected.

Grace accepts us even when emotions aren't pretty.

Precious Jesus, Lamb of God who takes away my sin and shame, thank You for placing me in a safe relationship with the Father. Thank You that in His culture of grace I am never condemned or rejected for negative emotion. This freedom makes my heart swell with joy.

Day 3: Marvelous Grace

Marvelous, infinite, matchless grace,
Freely bestowed on all who believe!
You that are longing to see His face,
Will you this moment His grace receive?
> *"Grace Greater Than Our Sin," Text by*
> *Julia H. Johnston, Verse 4*

Before I understood grace, life was about working hard to be good enough for God and others. A black and white life, it was based upon my perception of right and wrong, the culture I was raised in, and my life experiences.

Some people take it a step further. They believe being a good person and doing acts of kindness guarantees eternity in heaven. They work to put enough points on a cosmic tally sheet to balance the bad of their lives.

In my case, working hard to please God made me easy prey. People could tell me I wasn't good enough or point out my mistakes, and I'd bend over backwards to live up to their expectations. I often chose my activities based on a bogus list of expectations. I thought God and others embraced or pushed me away based upon my performance. I was kept in a state of hungering for conditional acceptance.

Some people tweak this thinking a little. They take up a cause and work hard, in an effort to justify the bad in them by giving themselves to the service of mankind. They, too, are easy victims. As they perform a calculated word can trick them into a tailspin. They respond similarly to the way I did, seeking to be accepted by God and others based upon their lists of accomplishments or good deeds.

It's a no win situation.

Deep down we know we can never measure up. We'll eventually blow it—sometime, somewhere.

God's grace offers a better way. Jesus washes us clean. The fancy Bible word is justified. I love the old church camp explanation for the word justification: "just as if I'd never sinned."

Christ's justification allows us to live from a position of victory. We already have the complete, unconditional acceptance of the Father. We have nothing to earn. We no longer perform for approval.

John 3:17 says God sent Jesus to save us, not condemn us. John 3:18 continues, "Whoever believes in him is not condemned, but whoever does not believe is condemned already because he has not believed in the name of God's one and only Son" (NIV). The point of this Scripture is if we look to our own goodness we'll never be free of condemnation. It is by looking to the perfection of Christ and His willing sacrifice that we can step out of our own self-loathing.

God's mercy extends to all people, offering an escape from guilt. His mercy welcomes each to draw near to His heart and discover how it feels to be set completely free from all our faults. He simply says, "Come. Hand me the keys to your life. Accept my grace."

God's multifaceted grace frees us from condemnation and welcomes us into His family. It brings us into relationship with God, and then transforms us from the inside out. We discover a great desire to be all He wants us to be. Slowly, we stop beating ourselves up and trust Him to change us. Once we invite Him into our lives, we seek to follow Him, one step at a time, making choices based on His will and not the approval of others.

As the season of Easter draws near, I encourage you to examine yourself. Do others easily manipulate you? Do you make choices trying to earn God acceptance or people's approval? Are you a control freak, trying to make your world perfect? These struggles hint to a need for a deepened understanding of grace.

In great mercy Jesus stands before us, arms of love outstretched, longing to welcome us into emotional rest. Grace is free, full, and for the asking.

Father, please help me accept Your forgiveness which frees me from the bondage of sin and guilt. Open my heart to understand Your gift of grace and help me to respond to it anew.

Week Twelve ~ Celebrating Grace

Day 4: Dragon Scales and Grace

Dark is the stain that we cannot hide.
What can avail to wash it away?
Look! There is flowing a crimson tide.
Whiter than snow you may be today.
> ~ *"Grace Greater Than Our Sin," Text by*
> *Julia H. Johnston, Verse 3*

God in His grace doesn't leave us like we are. While His grace covers our sins, it is also His grace that changes us, transforming us into the image of Christ. And, sometimes, God's transforming grace works through pain.

In difficult seasons I prayed for intimacy with Christ and, though coming to know Him better, I also experienced hard times. Assault after assault left me frightened, and I began to shut down from God. I knew intimacy with Him meant being open, but I didn't invite the Lord into the situation. I feared more pain. A numb deadness covered me while depression threatened.

Finally, I asked a friend to pray with me. She confronted the lie—that I could ignore all that had happened and the resulting anger seething beneath the surface.

"You're hurting already," she pointed out. "Why not be real before God?"

I cried and poured my heart out to Jesus in the midst of a small circle of praying women.

Later, alone in the car, I tried to process the pain I'd admitted. "You know, God," I said, "sometimes getting to know you hurts like crazy. Intimacy with You can be very painful."

Instantly, a scene from a book in C.S. Lewis' *Chronicles of Narnia* series played through my mind.

A boy named Eustace sneaked into a dragon's lair to steal the jewels the beast guarded. Instead of claiming the treasure, Eustace's greed caused an enchantment to turn *him* into the *dragon*. Horrified, Eustace, trapped inside the dragon's body, pounded around the cave, trying to shed the horrible skin he now lived in. No matter what He did Eustace couldn't shed the ugly dragon scales. In desperation, he finally called to Alsan, the Christ figure in the book. The majestic lion bounded into the cave and ever so lovingly came to the boy's rescue.

But the process was painful.

Layer after layer of dragon skin had to be ripped away by Aslan's sharp claws before the boy could be free of the shell that held him captive.

As I remembered the story, the Lord whispered to my heart, "It's not intimacy with me that hurts, Paula. It's getting rid of the old skin that enslaves you."

Like Eustace, tough, thick scales, caused by my own sins and lies from the enemy, covered the real me. My loving Lord came to the rescue, allowing pain that ultimately resulted in His purposes—the shedding of another layer of outward scum and the revealing of the person He is making me to be.

I chose to go to that raw, angry, tired place I was afraid of. I spat out my accusations against the Lord and cried for mercy, begging Him to carry me to faith and truth once more. In this process, I had to be honest before Him and see where that took me. I had to give Him permission to extend a strong, sharp claw and rip away the stain of sin in my life.

For a while it felt I'd gone backward in my walk of faith—frustrated by doubts, anger, and fears. But when I emerged on the other side of the season, I realized I'd only gone deeper in my relationship with the Lord.

During this time a phrase from a song sung by Sara Groves ministered to my heart. "And in His hands, the pain and hurt feels less like scars and more like character."

I'm glad God ripped away that yucky old layer of scales. I have no doubt but that in His perfect time, He'll tackle yet another rough place.

Thank God His grace never leaves us in old skin. God slowly and patiently pulls it away, revealing new, pink skin beneath, and we emerge as the new person He has seen all along.

Thank You for making me a new creation in You. Give me the courage to enter into the seasons that help me shed old skin, remembering in Your hands the pain and hurt is less like scars and more like character. Thank You for always seeing the amazing me I'm becoming but can't see and for Your commitment to make sure that transformation takes place.

Week Twelve ~ Celebrating Grace
Day 5: Polishing Grace

Marvelous grace of our loving Lord.
Grace that exceeds our sin and our guilt!
Yonder on Calvary's mount outpoured,
There where the blood of the Lamb was spilt.
> ~ *"Grace Greater Than Our Sin," Text by*
> *Julia H. Johnston, Verse 1*

And after you have suffered for a little while, the God of all grace,
who called you to His eternal glory in Christ, will Himself perfect,
confirm, strengthen, and establish you.
> ~ *I Peter 5:10 (NASB)*

Sometimes people get nervous when talking about grace.
They're concerned to fully rely on God's forgiving grace
gives us a license to ignore our faults. But living in a rule
driven state doesn't make us holy, either. Focusing on rules
almost always results in guilt from failure or pride from
success, neither of which is conducive to experiencing
consistency in our relationship with God. Sometimes, trying
really hard to be good actually puts so much focus on sin

that we grow worse instead of better! Rule-focused living also makes it hard for us to be graceful in our relationships with other people.

As Christ-followers we want to be holy. Some people think we're left with two options—to accept Christ's forgiving grace and believe He covers our sin (and give up on change) or to work really hard to live a holy life by following all the rules and make ourselves change (which sets us up for either obvious failure or outward performance without inner transformation).

There is another way.

My dear friend since childhood, Caryl Kirtley, told me a story that illustrates this. She wrote: "For hours I painstakingly worked to get all the years of tarnish off the silver I inherited. While I scrubbed God gave me an 'aha.' We're like that silver. We have areas that aren't too tarnished; areas that are so tarnished, deep in the crevices, that it seems we will never be beautiful again; and in-between areas. Overall, not a pretty sight! BUT when we give ourselves over to Him, He works on those places— removing the tarnish and leaving a beautiful patina—more beautiful than we imagined possible. And it's not a one-time process. No matter how immaculate we try to remain we live in a dirty world that inevitably gets on us. Just like silver, not kept pure and clean, we find ourselves in His hands many times over as He removes new tarnish."

Her words illustrate how fully God is the One who polishes us. Like a set of silver we can't get all the tarnish off ourselves. It takes an Outside Source.

This story illustrates another truth: Silver is always silver. Its worth is unchanged before or after the tarnish is wiped away, but when silver is polished its beauty increases.

Caryl says the more frequently she places herself in the Father's hands, the less severe the polishing job. Her thoughts remind me that the real answer to my failure is continuous surrender.

And even in that, there is grace.

On my own, I often struggle to submit to His polishing cloth. Sometimes the best I can do is to pray He'll make me willing. In these times, I'm encouraged by the words in Philippians 2:13, "For God is working in you, giving you the desire to obey him and the power to do what pleases him" (NLT).

As I surrender to His cleaning it is not my innate worth at stake—that was already purchased at the cross.

He's simply making me shine.

I try to be patient with myself. The Father will rub the tarnish off one area quickly, but another area may take more time. In His mercy, He doesn't scrub some places until He knows I'm up to the polishing.

Malachi 3:3 tells us God is "as a refiner and purifier of silver" (KJV). We can trust Him as the Master Designer of our life. My friend left one piece of her silver tarnished. When placed next to those she polished, it's a visible reminder of God's work. He continually polishes us, making us shine.

Wow! Thank You for making me shine. Give me the desire and ability to surrender to Your polishing cloth, and help me to believe Your work really does reveal a beautiful patina in my life.

Week Thirteen ~ Crucifixion Community

Week Thirteen ~ Crucifixion Community

Day 1: Alone

Stay here and keep watch with me.
~ Matthew 26:38 (NIV)

When the credits rolled on the black and white classic, "*An Affair to Remember*," my daughter and I heaved a contented sigh. I wiped a few sentimental tears from my cheeks and went about my evening.

As the night continued I wondered why the heroine was determined go it alone. If she really loved the hero, why didn't she show her weakness and admit her need? Do we Americans think there's some kind of virtue in carrying everything by ourselves?

Then it hit me.

I've often responded like she did. I hid in times of neediness, even from closest friends and family. Sometimes I don't share pain because I'm ashamed. Pride rears its ugly head within me, and I want to veil my weakness. Other times I don't want to burden my loved ones, especially when I know they can't fix the problem.

This isn't the example Jesus set for me. In His greatest

hour of need where did He turn? To His Father and His best friends. Remember the Garden of Gethsemane? He took his buddies there with Him on the night of His betrayal. He wanted them nearby.

But He didn't just stop there. He asked His closest friends, Peter, James, and John, to enter more deeply into His struggle. He told them, "My soul is overwhelmed with sorrow to the point of death. Stay here and keep watch with me" (Matthew 26:38, NIV).

With His friends nearby Jesus then poured His heart out to His Father.

It's interesting Jesus didn't sneak off to be alone and pray as He often did. In this time of great emotional anguish, He stayed near those who loved Him best. He knew they couldn't fix what was happening to Him. The trial had to be faced. But, being fully human, He wanted companionship in His time of greatest need.

If Jesus needed His closest friends nearby in time of pain who are we to think we can go it alone?

Jesus, thank You for Your example of reaching out to those closest to us in times of need. Help me to let go of pride and share with someone I trust when my heart is heavy. Thank You for putting people in my life who will stay put and keep watch with me during the difficult times.

Week Thirteen ~ Crucifixion Community

Day 2: Friendship

Rejoice with those who rejoice [sharing others' joy], and weep with those who weep [sharing others' grief].
    ~ Romans 12:15 (AMP)

Life has a way of changing. Like ocean waves lapping upon a shore, it is constant, but in continual ebb and flow. In the midst of the shifting of life, our relationships change as well. Schedules that used to fit together no longer mesh. Friendships once tight drift apart.

   This happened in my community. The people I spent time with no longer did the same things I did. My friends and I rushed about meeting the needs of the new era of our lives. We didn't take time to play together. There were no more conversations at the park while the children frolicked. Laughter and shared life experience didn't pass between us as often as it once did. Gradually, our intimacy diminished.

   One day I really needed my friends, and I couldn't find them. A long, persistent trial drained me, and I longed for someone to walk with me over the long haul. I wanted a few women who could weep with me. Oh, I had friends I could admit a hard day's struggle to, but no one that I felt I could share my on-going pain with. I hadn't been laughing, playing, or talking with friends. How could I ask them to weep with me, not just once, but often?

Yesterday we talked about how Jesus asked His closest friends to stay with Him in His hour of greatest need. What strikes me about that story is Jesus and His best friends had spent three years in each other's company. They ate meals together. They laughed and experienced life together. They rejoiced in exalted moments as they saw God bring miracles into their world.

They lived in community.

When Jesus said, "My soul is overwhelmed with sorrow to the point of death. Stay here and keep watch with me" (Matthew 26:38, NIV). He asked as someone who had walked through both joys and sorrows with His friends. He could request their presence in His darkest hour because sharing life was normal for them.

The New Testament church took community seriously. They knew that while God could be found through personal prayer and Scripture reading, they were healthier when they functioned as a body. They were encouraged to rejoice and weep together. They were told to love one another and care for each other's needs.

During my season of neediness, I was convicted to slow down and make a commitment to community. The Lord showed me that it was okay to allow friendships their season, but that it wasn't okay to live without a few people to whom I could be vulnerable. I needed people who I laughed and cried with.

The Lord also showed me I needed to allow Him to lead my friendships—weaning me from some, building closeness with others. He impressed upon me the need for balance, that it was important to take time to play, laugh, and live life, not just conquer an overwhelming to-do list. I also needed to look at my own needs as important as my children's. How many times had I driven them to a friend's house or even hosted a whole gaggle of kids but not had my friends over?

I don't completely understand community, but I'm trying to make changes that are more in-line with Christ's example. And now, I need to wrap this devotion up so I can get to bed. I need to get up early tomorrow.

I'm having breakfast with a friend!

Jesus, thank You for Your example of intimate friendship. Help me value my friends by giving proper space for those relationships You want me to develop further. Help me let go of friendships when it is time and to hold onto those that should stay. Please give me safe friends who help me know You better and help me be a safe friend, too.

Week Thirteen ~ Crucifixion Community

Day 3: Betrayed

I tell you the truth, one of you will betray me.
~ Matthew 26:21 (NLT)

Have you ever been courageously vulnerable only to be hurt?

Most of us have.

Yesterday I mentioned how I hid my pain. When I finally summoned the strength to share more openly, a well-meaning friend said EXACTLY the WRONG thing. I thought, "Oh, yeah. This is why I quit sharing." Temptation to crawl back into my private place and shut out my community was strong. Thankfully, I felt safe enough with this friend to explain my perspective on the situation, and we agreed to disagree.

A couple of months ago I did the opposite. I emailed a close friend with a vulnerable, private prayer request. I didn't hear back from her—no email, no phone call, nothing! When I saw her a few days later, I didn't have the guts to speak with her about it. I pretended everything was fine, but hurt coursed through me. I'd been courageously vulnerable only to be ignored. I found out later she never received that email. I could have saved myself weeks of pain and built up my friendship instead of letting it languish if I'd risked an honest conversation with her.

Often, honest communication and a bit of risk-taking is all a relationship needs to thrive and overcome difficulty. But, as we all have experienced, sometimes it doesn't matter how hard we try. We still get hurt. Relationships don't heal. The other person chooses to move on.

So what do we do when we seek to enter community as Jesus modeled for us, but we find that being vulnerable brings pain?

As I meditate on that question, a scene from the last supper comes to mind. Jesus is sitting with His closest friends, His twelve disciples. He shares Passover with them. Right before He institutes the taking of the Lord's Supper, He remarks that one of his friends will betray him.

Judas says, "Is it I?"

Jesus says, "It's you." He doesn't play games, but gives a direct answer. There is no record that He said anything further—no accusations, anger, trying to persuade otherwise. Just honest communication.

You'd think that would be enough betrayal for one night, but after the Passover celebration ended Jesus and His friends go to the Mount of Olives to the Garden of Gethsemane. As they walk Jesus tells His friends that all of them will desert him. Peter argues, but Jesus knows the truth. Even His best friends will leave Him when the going gets rough.

I think it is interesting that even in this knowledge, He invites his friends to be close to Him, as we talked about in the first devotional of this series.

As I'm thinking about the times my friends have betrayed me—or I have betrayed them—I see two kinds of betrayal. There is a Judas betrayal and a Peter betrayal. Both betrayals come from a weakness of character, a lack of understanding the big picture, and a spiritual immaturity.

The difference is the heart.

Judas's betrayal was premeditated. Instead of repenting and trying to make it right with Jesus, he took away all chance of reconciliation.

Peter's betrayal came from a heart that was weak but full of love. Peter grieved his actions, repented, and accepted forgiveness. He hung near to Jesus even in Christ's death, still hoping for reconciliation. He didn't give up.

Jesus forgave them both, but Judas He allowed to go on his way, knowing the relationship was severed. Peter He pursued—both before and after his betrayal.

Perhaps, herein lies the answer to our question. When intimate, vulnerable relationships bring pain and the people we trust betray us, we can follow Christ's example.

First, we communicate honestly and refuse to play games as we navigate the difficult waters. Then, we forgive as He forgave. Knowing that Jesus, too, has felt the deep pain of betrayal, we then go to Him for comfort in the confidence that we have a Savior who understands. As we let Him minister to our wounds, we also seek His counsel. He can show us whether to pursue the relationship or let it go.

Jesus, I'm sad You, too, walk through the pain of being hurt by those closest to You, but it also brings me comfort because I know You truly understand how I feel when I'm betrayed. I'm glad I can come to You when I walk through a painful relationship. I know

Awaken

You will understand, minister to my heart and show me how to respond.

You may appreciate reading Matthew 26 and John 21 as you meditate on these thoughts.

Week Thirteen ~ Crucifixion Community

Day 4: Unity

I am praying not only for these disciples but also for all who will ever believe in me because of their testimony. My prayer for all of them is that they will be one, just as you and I are one, Father— that just as you are in me and I am in you, so they will be in us, and the world will believe you sent me.
   ~ John 17:20–21 (NLT)

"Wow! Jesus prayed for ME!" Excited, I wrote a note in the margin of my Bible so I'd always remember John 17:20–26 was prayed with me in mind. This happened several years ago.

What strikes me about this Scripture is two things. First, Christ's precious prayer related to community. He prayed I would be one with the Father and Him, and I would be one with fellow Christians. Jesus said it was this spiritual unity that would cause other people to believe in Him.

The second thing that makes this prayer especially meaningful is that it is sandwiched between two very important events—the Lord's Supper and Jesus' betrayal in the garden.

Amazing. As Jesus prepared to face the cruelty of the cross, He thought of me—and you.

In Christ's most difficult hour He thought about the unity He shared with His Father and wanted to share with us. He focused not only on community with His disciples, but on the community of the ages—the connection between Jesus and you and me and people to come.

Later when Jesus hangs upon the cross, we see Him continue to focus on relationship. The gospels record seven phrases that Jesus spoke from the cross. Five of the seven have to do with relationship.

Jesus spoke with the thieves who hung on either side of Him.

He prayed that God would forgive those who crucified Him.

He asked the beloved disciple to care for His mother.

He prayed to His Father. Two of the most oft repeated phrases of the cross connected Him to eternal community. He quoted David's words from the Psalms when He cried, "My God, My God, why have You forsaken me?" and again when he prayed, "Father, into your hands I commit My spirit." Christ's words spanned centuries of relationship.

Jesus knew His sacrifice would bring about wonderful, magnificent changes in the area of community. When He spoke His final words, "It is finished," and breathed His last breath, the curtain in the temple that separated people from the presence of God was ripped in two.

God is now accessible, living in community with His people for eternity. His followers—past, present, and future—were suddenly and forever connected to Him, without the barriers of the old covenant.

We are connected to the Trinity now and through that connection to all those who have gone before us and will come after us. Someday we will experience this in fullness. King David, Jesus, the disciples, and the believers to come—all living in perfect unity, joyfully worshiping the Father. We'll stand side by side with Moses, your great-grandmother, Martin Luther, Queen Esther, Uncle Joe, Nate Saint, and even that Christian with whom you can't see eye to eye. All differences will fade in the unity of the Spirit and all relationships will be perfect and whole.

The prize set before Christ when He chose to be sacrificed for you and me was *us*.

Christ suffered because He knew eternity together would be worth momentary pain. At the great wedding feast of the Lamb and His bride, the joyous celebration will focus on the fact that nothing will ever again keep us apart.

God died to unify us with Himself—and each other—forever.

Father, Son, and Holy Spirit, I'm awestruck at the thought of eternity in perfect, intimate community with You. Thank You, Father, for sending Jesus. Thank You, Jesus, for enduring the cross so we live together. Forever.

Week Thirteen ~ Crucifixion Community

Day 5: Forever

As they entered the tomb, they saw a young man dressed in a white robe sitting on the right side, and they were alarmed. "Don't be alarmed," he said. "You are looking for Jesus the Nazarene, who was crucified. He has risen! He is not here. See the place where they laid him. But go, tell his disciples and Peter, 'He is going ahead of you into Galilee. There you will see him, just as he told you.'"
    ~ Mark 16: 5–7 (NLT)

I awoke with an old hymn playing through my mind. "Christ the Lord is risen today. Alleluia." My heart sang. "Son of men and angels say: Alleluia! Raise your joys and triumphs high, Alleluia! Sing ye heav'ns, and earth reply: Alleluia!"

Much to my husband's surprise, I burst out in song from beneath the covers. "Alleluia!"

But I don't believe Mary Magdalene, Salome, and Mary the mother of James awoke quite that way just over 2000 years ago. The night before, the women had gone out after sundown to purchase spices to anoint Christ's body.

There was no joyous song in their heart as they walked to the tomb the next morning.

In fact, I imagine they both dreaded and anxiously awaited the task before them—rubbing the cold, lifeless, hardened body of their beloved Jesus with spices. It was to be a final act of love, their last connection with Him.

I can almost feel the heaviness of their steps as they walked to His grave worrying over how they would move the heavy stone from its entrance. Their pace must have quickened, then slowed. How they longed to honor Him—how they loathed this final good-bye.

But a surprise awaited them.

Instead of a lifeless body, an empty tomb and a glowing man in a white robe greeted them. The angel told them Jesus had risen. "But go," said the angel, "tell his disciples and Peter, 'He is going ahead of you into Galilee. There you will see him, just as he told you.'"

The angel could have had any message for Jesus' friends that day. He could have told them the theological implications of the resurrection. He could have chided them for their lack of faith. A long recounting of prophecy fulfilled could have flown from his lips.

But his message basically said, "He's alive, and He wants to see you in Galilee! Tell His best friends, especially Peter, who's still beating himself up over his betrayal of Jesus, that the Lord wants to be with you guys!"

Christ rose, and He wanted to see His friends. That's the kind of Lord we serve.

Jesus is a glorious, powerful, magnificent Lord to be sure, but in His glory He is not distant, domineering, or untouchable. Our God is One who wants to be with us. Emmanuel.

Scripture tells us Jesus died to reconcile us to the Father and to Himself. He allowed Himself to be separated from His friends because He wanted to be even closer to them. He tore down the wall of sin that had long kept Him from His creation so we could grow in intimacy and come to know our God as our Best Friend. Just as He promised in John 14, He who had walked *with* them would now live *in* them.

Community with Jesus is forever and always. We begin our friendship with Him here and continue it for eternity. The same is true for relationship with our friends who discover His embrace. Ours is a bond that will never be broken. As precious as our communion is with Him and His people today, a brighter day will come when we, too, will taste the power of resurrection. We will join with our loved ones who've gone before us in spending eternity with our Best Friend.

Hallelujah! He is risen indeed! Risen to be close to us forever, never to be separated.

Praise You, Jesus! King of Kings and Lord of Lords! All creation cries out in joyous adoration. You have risen! Hallelujah! Risen to walk in power and majesty. Risen to welcome us into the throne room. Risen to be my Friend forever. Hallelujah!

Acknowledgments

This book is a miracle. Special thanks to each of you who prayed it into being, especially my husband (Jerry), the Council (Deborah Besaw, Jill Hups, Kathy Kovach, and Marjorie Vawter), and my friend Li.

A 2015 Christmas miracle (which is what I call the release of *Soul Scents: Awaken*) happened because several angels answered God's prompting to see this through to publication. Without your selfless giving and incredible giftedness this book would not exist.

Special thanks to Carmen Barber, project manager, software genius, and author whisperer. Your organization, understanding of tools, and ability to network were part of this from the beginning. Your calm encouragement and can-do attitude was just what Jesus knew I needed. Thank you. Without your vision for the processes in making this happen I'd still be staring at a jumble of Word documents. I'm honored to call you friend.

Lisa-Joy, gifted artist and deep, beautiful woman, I still feel a little breathless at how you drank tea at my kitchen table on the exact day I was asking the Lord if it was time to release book one. When you offered your artwork, it was the confirmation I needed to move forward. Every step of the way you served this project with grace and passion, and when I saw how you brought my message to life in art, my heart sang. You are a dear woman, and I love our growing friendship.

Kim Liddiard of the Creative Pixel, I've always known you were part genius. Few people possess the ability to get lost in the creative right side of their brain one minute and write computer code the next. You are truly gifted. Thank you for fitting my project in your busy schedule. Even if you weren't my long-time friend you'd be the cover designer I wanted! You immediately caught the vision for this series and patiently helped shape my confused preferences into a collection I love. You are a blessing!

Ruth Meyers, editor and all around English champ, thank you not only for pouring yourself forth in service in such a timely manner, but also for speaking grace into me as you did it. Your text partway through the project brought tears to my eyes and helped me believe this book could truly touch hearts. Thank you for the constant support and friendship. You are a treasure.

Margie Vawter, you came along when I needed a final line edit/proofread, and you taught me more than I knew I didn't know! Ha! You are not only one of my dearest and most valuable friends and prayer-partners, you are the great *CMS* rescuer! I will never forget your generosity.

Jerry Moldenhauer, you have always been my biggest cheerleader (outside of God himself). Your understanding of business, willingness to research the stuff I don't want to think about, and never-ending support for my dreams gives me wings. Thank you for years of working alongside me. Remember the old days when we did the weekly devotional? You helped me refine my thoughts and saw that they reached *Soul Scents* subscribers. The journey of publication of this series can be traced back to a day over ten years ago when we walked through the neighborhood, and you challenged me to start my own devotional website. Initially I told you I was too busy writing novels and homeschooling *your* children to add one more thing. But God's Spirit and your gentle guidance won me over and sent me on one of the best journeys of my life. If you and Jesus didn't believe in me I don't know that I would be writing today. In the hard times when I wanted to rush off for more stable employment and income, you constantly redirected me to the job God called me to, never complaining about my contribution (or lack thereof) to the family's financial coffers. Thank you for giving me my dreams—both to be home with *our* children and to become the writer and speaker God is calling me to be.

Thank you to Sarah, Seth, Stephen, and Sam for being children who constantly delight my heart. Thank you for your patience as I zoned at the computer for large chunks of your childhood and for letting me write about you all these years as our interactions taught me more about Jesus. Sarah, you challenge me to brave, and you tell me you're proud of me. What a gift! Seth, you've offered grace beyond what I deserved and reminded me to receive it from the Grace-giver. Thank you. And Stephen and Sam—you have no idea how wonderful it is for a mom to have adult sons pray for her. Thank you, Stephen, for all those phone calls that ended with, "Can I pray for you, Mom?" and thank you, Sam, for the times you took my hand and asked the Lord to help me write well and conquer my projects. I couldn't be more joyful and proud of the adults you four have become. Thank you, too, for bringing David, Amanda, and Ariel into our family journey. You kids have great taste in spouses and girlfriends!

I can't begin to list everyone who encouraged me on my writing journey, but of special mention are Marlene Bagnull of the Colorado Christian Writer's Conference who was the first professional to believe in me and who tenaciously encouraged me to keep pursuing the writing path; my beautiful agent, Rachelle Gardner who speaks kindness and wisdom as she cheers me on; and Brandilyn Collins, author extraordinaire and ACFW board member who prayed me through some of the hardest years ever.

In 2004 many of you began reading *Soul Scents* devotionals. Over the years the subscription list grew to a few thousand. Thank you to each one who journeyed with me in those years becoming a *Soul Scents* friend. Many of the devotionals in this collection were written all those years ago, and the truths the Lord placed into our hearts then are just as true today. I'm honored to have walked with you as we entered more deeply into our Savior's heart.

And to you, my new readers. Thank you for desiring Jesus and allowing me space in your journey.

About the Author

Author, speaker, and mom of four, Paula Moldenhauer encourages others to be released into their full potential through freedom in Christ and the empowerment of God's grace. She has published over 300 times in the non-fiction market.

To book Paula to speak at your next event, contact her at Paula@PaulaMoldenhauer.com.
Speaking topics can be found on her website:
www.paulamoldenhauer.com

Paula's first full length novel, *Titanic: Legacy of Betrayal*, is available on Kindle. Co-authored with Kathleen E. Kovach, this book tells the story of a young real estate agent whose life is affected by a century-old deception.

> ~ *A secret. A key. Much was buried when the Titanic went down, but now it's time for resurrection.*

Paula's novella, *You're a Charmer, Mr. Grinch*, included in the collection *Postmark: Christmas,* was an ACFW Carol Award finalist.

Awaken

Lisa-Joy's Artwork

Lisa-Joy invites you to her Facebook page
www.facebook.com/lisajoyart to see her illustrations, letter art,
and coloring book page designs. She begins each work by
hand thereby creating its clean, optimistic style. Contact
Lisa-Joy at lisajoyart@gmail.com.

Awaken

Soul Scents **Collection**

Thank you for taking this spiritual journey with *Soul Scents: Awaken*. This is the first book in a series of devotions.

To see information on the next three *Soul Scents* devotional volumes, Paula's current list of speaking and conference topics, blog and more, visit: www.paulamoldenhauer.com

Made in the USA
San Bernardino, CA
30 April 2016